# Buddha, Ch
## Three Wise Me

*by*

### Christopher Penczak

**COPPER**
**CAULDRON**
PUBLISHING

# Credits

**Editing:** Steve Kenson, James St. Onge
**Proofreading:** Mary Ellen Darcy, James St. Onge
**Cover Design:** Derek Yesman/Daydream Design
**Interior Art:** Christopher Penczak
**Layout & Publishing:** Steve Kenson

For more information visit:
*www.christopherpenczak.com*
*www.coppercauldronpublishing.com*

ISBN 978-0-9827743-4-2, First Printing

Printed in the U.S.A.

# Acknowledgements

Special thanks to Stephanie Rutt for teaching me how to relate to the Eastern Traditions and amazing yoga classes; to R.J. Stewart for his scholarly and groundbreaking work into the true magic of Merlin, Raven Grimassi and Stephanie Taylor Grimassi for all their wonderful magical conversations and advice; Chris Giroux for his ever wise insights; my partners Steve and Adam; my father Ronald; my mother Rosalie; and my amazing community.

# Other Books by Christopher Penczak

*City Magick* (Samuel Weiser, 2001)

*Spirit Allies* (Samuel Weiser, 2002)

*The Inner Temple of Witchcraft* (Llewellyn Publications, 2002)

*The Inner Temple of Witchcraft* CD Companion (Llewellyn Publications, 2002)

*Gay Witchcraft* (Samuel Weiser, 2003)

*The Outer Temple of Witchcraft* (Llewellyn Publications, 2004)

*The Outer Temple of Witchcraft* CD Companion (Llewellyn Publications, 2004)

*The Witch's Shield* (Llewellyn Publications, 2004)

*Magick of Reiki* (Llewellyn Publications, 2004)

*Sons of the Goddess* (Llewellyn Publications, 2005)

*The Temple of Shamanic Witchcraft* (Llewellyn Publications, 2005)

*The Temple of Shamanic Witchcraft* CD Companion (Llewellyn Publications, 2005)

*Instant Magick* (Llewellyn Publications, 2005)

*The Mystic Foundation* (Llewellyn Publications, 2006)

*Ascension Magick* (Llewellyn Publications, 2007)

*The Temple of High Witchcraft* (Llewellyn Publications, 2007)

*The Temple of High Witchcraft* CD Companion (Llewellyn Publications, 2007)

*The Living Temple of Witchcraft* Volume I (Llewellyn Publications, 2008)

*The Living Temple of Witchcraft* Volume I CD Companion (Llewellyn Publications, 2008)

*The Living Temple of Witchcraft* Volume II (Llewellyn Publications, 2009)

*The Living Temple of Witchcraft* Volume II CD Companion (Llewellyn Publications, 2009)

*The Witch's Coin* (Llewellyn Publications, 2009)

*The Three Rays of Witchcraft* (Copper Cauldron Publishing, 2010)

*The Plant Spirit Familiar* (Copper Cauldron Publishing, 2010)

*The Witch's Heart* (Llewellyn Publications, 2011)

*The Gates of Witchcraft* (Copper Cauldron Publishing, 2012)

# Table of Contents

LIST OF FIGURES...............................................................8

CHAPTER 1: THE THREE WISE MEN.............................................9

CHAPTER 2: THE THREE DIVINE FORCES....................................17

CHAPTER THREE: A NEW VISION...........................................25

CHAPTER FOUR: THE WAY OF THE BUDDHA .............................33

CHAPTER FIVE: THE JOURNEY OF CHRIST ...............................43

CHAPTER SIX: THE MISSION OF MERLIN..................................53

CHAPTER SEVEN: THE PRACTICES OF BUDDHISM .....................63

    The Three Jewels.............................................64

    The World of the Buddhists..............................64

    Liberation......................................................67

    The Teachings of the Buddha.............................69

        *The Four Noble Truths* .................................69

        *The Noble Eightfold Path* .............................70

    The Practice of Buddhism..................................72

        *Mindfulness*..............................................73

        *Inviting the Bell*.........................................74

        *Breath Meditation* .....................................75

        *Chanting*..................................................76

        *Devotion* .................................................78

        *Altars of Veneration* ...................................78

        *Incense Offering* ........................................79

        *Zen Koan* ................................................79

        *Bodhisattva Vow*........................................80

    The Dalai Lama and Tibet..................................82

    Tantric & Mystical Buddhism .............................83

        *Assuming the Form of Avalokiteśvara*.............86

CHAPTER EIGHT: THE HEART OF CHRISTIANITY .......................91

    The Code of Christ..........................................92

        *Love* .......................................................94

        *The Golden Rule*........................................96

*Non-Violence* ...............................................................................97

*Forgiveness* ...............................................................................98

*Charity* .......................................................................................99

*Poverty* .....................................................................................101

*Humility* ...................................................................................102

*Chastity* ....................................................................................103

*Diligence* ..................................................................................104

*Trust* .........................................................................................105

Traditional Concepts of Mainstream Christianity ...........106

*Sin, Sacrifice, and Redemption* .............................................107

The Rituals of Christianity ......................................................115

*Prayer* ........................................................................................116

*Baptism* ....................................................................................120

*Eucharist* ..................................................................................122

*Healing* .....................................................................................125

**CHAPTER NINE: THE WAY OF MAGIC**...............................................**129**

Defining Magic...........................................................................130

*Will* .............................................................................................133

*Communication*........................................................................136

*Consciousness* ..........................................................................138

The Way of Magic ......................................................................138

*The Principles of Magic Rituals*..............................................140

*Sacred Space and Time* ............................................................141

*The Four Powers* .......................................................................141

*Symbolism* .................................................................................142

*Correspondence* ........................................................................143

*The Moon* ..................................................................................144

Making Magic..............................................................................145

*Building an Altar* ......................................................................145

*Meditative State* .......................................................................146

*Ritual Space and Time*.............................................................146

*Spell* ...........................................................................................146

*Release* .......................................................................................147

*Divination* .................................................................................148

Immanence in Divinity .............................................................152

*Speaking to Nature*...................................................................154

The Wheel of the Year .............................................................. 155

    *Stewardship* .................................................................... *157*

CHAPTER TEN: UNITING THE THREE WAYS IN OUR AGE............................**159**

GLOSSARY................................................................................**171**

ABOUT THE AUTHOR .................................................................**184**

# List of Figures

Figure 1: Star of Bethlehem ............................................................45

Figure 2: Om Mani Padme Hum (Tibetan Characters)...............76

Figure 3: Vajra or Dorje ................................................................85

Figure 4: Avalokiteśvara ...............................................................86

Figure 5: Traditional Tree of Life...............................................111

Figure 6: Tree of Life with Malkuth Exalted ............................112

Figure 7: Rosary Beads ................................................................118

Figure 8: The Magician Card from the Tarot.............................151

# Chapter 1: The Three Wise Men

When I was a child, my mother would put a Nativity scene beneath the tree at Christmas. We would carefully unpack the paper maché statues wrapped in newsprint, and arrange them beneath our tree on a red felt cloth. Baby Jesus, of course, would be in the center, crowned with a golden halo, flanked by his parents, Mary and Joseph. Around them we placed a wide range of townspeople, manger animals like sheep and camels, and a few angels. But the statues that always intrigued me were the Three Wise Men.

The Three Wise men were the "kings" who brought baby Jesus his birthday gifts, gifts of frankincense, myrrh and gold. Though I didn't understand their significance then, and asked my mother if baby Jesus wouldn't have enjoyed some toys more, they now remain three of my favorite spiritual "tools" in my own religious practices. Each has a particular spiritual gift to offer humanity.

Perhaps their gifts started the idea about giving gifts at Christmas, at least the Christian justification of it, for there were many other traditions dating from before the birth of Christ that have become a part of our Christmas celebrations. Best known is the popular use of evergreen trees for decoration, coming from earlier Pagan traditions.

The Three Wise Men were said to arrive after Christ's birth, and were signaled to his birth in their far off home in the East because of the alignment and rise of an illustrious star indicating that a great new king had been born. My favorite Christmas carol became *We Three Kings,* detailing their journey and purpose. Officially called *We Three Kings of Orient Are,* it was a later addition to Christmas celebrations, written in 1857 by Rev. John Henry Hopkins, but by the time I was born, it was deeply entrenched into American Christmas, at least in the Catholics of New England.

The song revealed some interesting tidbits about the Three Wise Men. I didn't understand all of these points at first, but as my love of Christianity waned in my teens and my exploration of the hidden and esoteric began, I remembered the Three Wise Men. The song gave me some clues about what I needed to discover.

First, they were not just old men out for a ride. They were kings. But kings of what and where? They are from the Orient – Asia, east of where Jesus was born in Bethlehem. But why would three kings travel together, without their court? Were they regular kings, or kings of something else?

They focused on the star, the *"star of wonder, star of night, star of royal beauty bright."* They were stargazers and knew the importance of the stars to indicate what was occurring on the Earth.

Lastly, they brought three gifts – gold, frankincense and myrrh. Gold was to "crown" him as Jesus would be a king as well. But he, like these Three Wise Men, had no real nation-state, but a spiritual sovereignty that went beyond the boarders of nations, despite what his later supporters wanted him to be, a political — not spiritual— messiah.

Frankincense is a resin burned to raise the spirit, used in temples for prayers and praise of the divine. It is said to clear and uplift a space to bring it closer to the divine, and clear away harmful energies. Eastern temples use it much like Native American practitioners might use sage, to "smudge" people and places to spiritually cleanse them.

The third and final gift was the resin of myrrh. Myrrh is a "bitter perfume" used as incense like frankincense, but without the brighter qualities. It is used in funerary rituals and played a strong role in Egyptian temple practices, to embalm and preserve mummies. Its blessing is protection and preservation. The song associated myrrh with a prophecy of Jesus' life with the lines, *"Sorrowing, sighing, bleeding, dying. Sealed in the stone-cold tomb."* Of course Hopkins' "prophecy" came over 1800 years after the death of Christ, but he correctly described the spiritual qualities of myrrh in the context of Christ's life.

In my later spiritual explorations, I continually asked my teachers at Catholic school, "Why?" I asked it about everything, and when I realized I wouldn't get the reason behind the traditions and actions, and only dogmatic party lines, I started to go elsewhere. The public library became a good friend to me, letting me explore all sorts of topics that wouldn't come up in school, particularly in regard to religion. By the time I graduated from an all-boys Catholic high school, I was well underway in my studies of the esoteric, continually asking why and sometimes even finding the answer — or at least a better question.

Included in some of my early questions were ones about the Three Wise Men who fascinated me as a child, the three eastern kings. I found out on my own that while Christian tradition normally accepted the three kings, because of the three gifts, they are cited in the Gospel of Matthew with no number given. The Gospel of Matthew refers to them as "Magi," a word translated to magician or sorcerer, and the King James Bible made them "wise men." While Magi is the root of our word magic, it also refers to a caste of priests in Persian culture. In the Zoroastrian tradition of Persia (present day Iran) the Magi were a caste of priests concerned with the stars, and known as astrologers. Magi is actually a Latinized form of the Greek word *magos,* taken from the Persian *magus.* The image of the Magi as Persian magicians is not far off, as their caste could be roughly equated as the Persian form of the Celtic Druid caste, another group of priest-magicians given high regard in their society. From the images of the Magi and Druids, real or imagined, we have drawn the popular image of the European magician, in robe, full of stars and moons, pointed hat and wand.

Later accounts attempted to name the Three Kings, but continuing the problems of Christianity, none of the major institutions could agree on the details. The Western Christian Church identifies them as Caspar, Melchior, and Balthasar, the names I first learned as a Catholic. The origin of these names comes from an Alexandrian manuscript in Greek. Syrian Christians call them Larvandad, Gushnasaph, and Hormisdas. While these names sound more Persian than the first three, we don't know if they are any more "correct." The Ethiopian Church names them Hor, Karsudan, and Basanater and the Armenian Christians name them Kagpha, Badadakharida, and Badadilma. Christians of various ethnicities originating in the Middle East and East cite a connection to one of the three kings, giving them an origin as far away as China or Tibet.

So these three men were not your usual royal visitors. They were spiritual practitioners of some sort, with a great understanding of the stars, the time they lived in, prophecy, and the magical properties of the gifts they carried. They originated in a land where such arts were respected by their society, and they came—individually or as ambassadors of their people—to see this new "king" without a throne.

The more I learned, the more fascinated I became. Several points about these kings, real or mythic, piqued my curiosity. First, here were these foreign king-magicians, visiting the Messiah of the Jews. They were not Jewish, nor were they practicing Judaism. Yet there was some understanding that crossed the lines of faith and culture. They could see truth beyond their own confines. The Wise Men were not necessarily giving up their own religious and cultural traditions in favor of following Christ. They simply attended, brought gifts, paid respect, and went home. But they saw truth—wisdom—beyond their borders without invalidating their own practice. They were my first experiences of someone looking at religion cross-culturally, even if obliquely. I'm sure with the rise of Christianity, they didn't all convert, nor did their descendants, but they could hold both views at the same time, in a more harmonious, global perspective.

Second, they knew secret and hidden things. That was my obsession, the hidden reasons behind everything. The Magi's story pointed to a tradition with knowledge most people of their time— and certainly most people in Jerusalem— did not have. They seemed to have a system for gaining new information, not just rely on the old. It was progressive and adaptable. That system included stargazing to know what was happening on our planet, and where to go to see it. They understood the occult properties of objects from the ancient world and valued them enough to bring them as gifts. Of course these objects also had monetary value in that time period, but if they were just bringing money, then I'm sure the gifts would have included all sorts of more durable treasures. But only three specific items were brought.

Third, as the Three Wise Men always seemed to teach in threes, they had a sense of confidence in themselves, their traditions, and purpose.

The previous two characteristics lent to this third, but in a time of fear and uncertainty, just as any human age is a time of fear and uncertainty, the Three Kings seemed to know who they were, what they were doing, where they were going, when they had to be there, and why.

How many of us can answer all those questions at the same time?

Who? What? Where? When? And Why? These are the questions of life.

Sometimes we can answer them on a small scale, in the moment, but the larger scale of our lifetime leaves us wondering. How rare it is to find someone guided by a view that is adaptable, that can be both large and small, practical and spiritual, able to answer such questions.

The Three Wise Men were guided by the Star of Bethlehem on that journey, and guided by the spiritual light, the understanding of the universe, that the star represents. They knew how to find their guiding star in any moment, not just astrologically, but I suspect internally as well. They knew the still inner voice, the inner light that guides us if we choose to listen and look.

While the outer and inner stars guide them, they in turn, become guides to us, as role models and inspiration. We seek to be wise women and wise men. When our consciousness transformed from the group mentality of the early Stone Age people into the consciousness of the individual, these questions arose. Not only are we on a community journey, we are also on the individual path, and each must walk it alone. We seek to answer the questions of life and put those answers into action.

Who am I?

What do I do?

Where am I now, where have I been, and where am I going? Where am I in the universe, spiritually as well as physically? What is my cosmology?

When do I need to do these things?

Why I am answering any of these questions? What is the larger purpose?

Much of our life is spent seeking out people, places, religions, teachers, jobs, and relationships that will answer those questions for us, yet few get those answers. Rather than asking others to answer these questions for us, we need to seek out those who answered the questions for *themselves*. We can't trust their answers to be our answers, but we can study their methods. How did they find their answers, and can their process, their wisdom, help us to answer our own questions and put those answers into action? Those who seek role models on the quests of life do far better than those who relinquish control to another.

In looking at our Three Wise Men, we have the images of royalty, priests, magicians, astrologers, foreign wisdom, stars, travel, and sacred gifts. While Caspar, Melchior, and Balthasar start us in our journey, their lives are pretty sparse beyond what we have just reviewed. Yet every age has its wise men and women. Rich and detailed lives give us much to ponder and put into practice.

The story of the Three Wise Men really is the story of Jesus of Nazareth, known as the Christ, and the religion of Christianity that rose up after his death. Christ's life is one of the most influential in our modern history, going on to change, for good or ill, the entire world. While the dogma that has grown up around him is less than helpful, accounts of his life, even when conflicting, can provide valuable wisdom. Christ and Christianity are the middle expression of the lineage of traditions known as the People of the Book, of the written "Abrahamic" scriptures. It starts with the Jewish traditions from which Jesus came and has continued onward with the Islamic traditions. Both have their wise men as well.

On the eastern side of the world, a figure that predates Jesus and has also considerably influenced how many think, behave, and believe is Buddha. From his teachings arose the various forms of Buddhism. While the stories are not the same, and their spiritual emphasis differs, their wisdom often runs parallel. Buddha has become the image of the wise man for many.

Lastly, less well known, with no religion named after him, is the archetypal standard bearer for the pre-Christian western traditions,

Merlin. He is the secret Druid-priest and prophet of the indigenous European traditions, and in many ways his most primal teachings are indicative of the tribal Pagan teachings predating both Christianity and Buddhism. Nature-based spiritual traditions from all across the world, from Europe to the Americas, Africa to Australia, all have common cause. They see the land as divine, the power of the four directions, and the important role, both political and spiritual, of the tribal leader, chief, or king. While many figures could be the face of these teachings, the figure of Merlin has survived, adapted, and evolved into a form recognized by most, rivaling Christ and Buddha in terms of recognition, though from secular and fictional sources, not necessarily religious sources.

These three wise men will be our guides. Each has something unique to offer. Each of their traditions has evolved an aspect of our global human consciousness. Let us learn what we can from them, and then we can answer our own questions of who, what, where, when, and why.

# Chapter 2: The Three Divine Forces

The number three plays an integral role in religions across the world. Three is considered a divine number. Well, *any* number can be considered divine. One is the number of unity, the Great Spirit. Two is duality; male and female; darkness and light; good and evil. But three is special; it implies a connection between polarity, shift, or movement.

Catholicism looks at the one God as a trinity – Father, Son, and Holy Spirit, although the Holy Spirit was once the Holy Ghost, and related esoterically to the Holy Shekinah, the feminine presence of God. So though few Catholics think about it, it's more like Father, Son, and Mother. Not so far from the Egyptian trinity of Osiris, Horus, and Isis. In Hinduism, the cosmic forces are also a trinity – Brahma the Creator, Vishnu the Preserver, and Shiva the Destroyer. Wicca views the divine as the Goddess, embodying the three phases of life – Maiden, Mother, and Crone. Even medieval alchemists saw the universe divided among three spiritual principles, named after three chemicals – Sulfur, Mercury, and Salt.

One of my favorite divisions of three comes from the spiritual traditions of Theosophy. Theosophy means God – *Theo*, Wisdom – *Sophy*, or *Sophia*. It is the study of divine wisdom and seeks to unite various spiritual traditions. It was originally a name of a small sect in the early post-Christian era, but the name was claimed by a very interesting woman named Helena P. Blavatsky for her own organization and teachings. She wrote several books, including *Isis Unveiled* and *The Secret Doctrine*, where she proposed a hierarchy of spiritual masters from several different traditions guided the world, and specifically her work. While Blavatsky was surrounded by controversy for much of her life, the basic idea of looking at the Tradition with at capitol "T" behind all the spiritual and esoteric traditions of the world, took hold. Other writers and teachers who philosophically inherited the ideas of Theosophy, if not the official title of the Theosophical Society, built upon her work and took it in other directions.

One of the key ideas to later develop out of these teaching was the concept of the light of the divine as divided into several "rays," like the colors of the rainbow. Each ray embodies a different archetypal force. The rays were divided into two categories, like primary and secondary colors. The primary rays are Red, Blue, and Yellow. The colors, ideas, and terminology around these rays changed over the decades, but the basic ideas of the three rays are the principles of Power, Love, and Wisdom.

Power is the First Ray, most often described as the Red Ray. The First Ray is fire, and life force. It is associated with sacred kings and Divine Will. Divine Will is a tough concept to understand. It's not the desire of the personality, the ego; that's will with a little "w." Divine Will is the Will of the soul, of the higher self, the part of you that is most like and in touch with the Creator. Individually, it is your soul's purpose. Collectively, it is the purpose of the universe, of all of creation. When people talk about God's plan, or Divine Providence, they are talking about Divine Will. In the human realm, it is the power to put the bigger picture, the true purpose, over human desires. But it works out best when we can align our personal desires with our soul's desires, and live our life from the perspective of our soul, not our personality. It doesn't mean we lose our personality, but the personality becomes a tool in life, rather than our sole identity. Divine Will helps us transcend our ego and work from a more enlightened perspective. Divine Will is Power, for when we are aligned with it, we are working in harmony with the creative power and anything is possible.

Love is the Second Ray. While many colors are associated with love, such as green and pink, in this system of three primary colors, the color of Divine Love is blue. The Blue Ray is the force of unconditional love, not personal and attached love. It is the uniting force, the connective energy that brings everything together.

Just as Divine Will is hard to understand, I think Divine Love is even harder. We live in a society that uses the word "love" for so many different emotions and situations. Ancient cultures, with a greater understanding of the energy of love, used different words to describe different kinds of love and relationships. The love between parents and children is different than between siblings. The love in a friendship is different from that of a marriage. They often cross over and intermingle, but they are different kinds of love.

So Divine Love is different from personal love. It is not attached. It does not expect. It is ever expansive and offered freely. If it is truly divine love, it does not retract in times of personal difficulty. It is unconditional. Yet unconditional love does not mean unconditional relationships. You can love someone unconditionally, but set personal boundaries to protect yourself from inappropriate behaviors. But the boundaries do not change the love. In fact, such boundaries make the love more possible. Many people think the key to enlightenment is this Divine Love. Not just having it for yourself, or for another, but when you truly tap into it, you begin to see this connective force between everyone. You see the beauty in everyone and everything, and love them, despite the personal situations or flaws. None of that matters to love. When everyone is loving everyone and everything else this way, we'll have heaven upon Earth.

Wisdom is the last of our triad. It is the energy of civilization because only with this wisdom and knowledge can we build what we think of as society. It gives "birth" to the four other colors, each relating to a human concept rather than a universal archetype – Green (Art), Orange (Science), Indigo (Religion), and Violet (Ritual).

Older traditions called this the Ray of Active Intelligence. What is active intelligence? Students of Theosophical lore question that phrase a lot. I know I did. I believe it means putting knowledge to use. What better definition of wisdom is there than knowing how and when to use something, and when not to use it? If humanity in general learned those two things, we'd collectively be far wiser than we are now, even though we probably have more intellectual knowledge, more information, now than in any previous era.

Divine Wisdom is true self-knowledge, knowledge of the mind and all of its contents as a tool. Like Divine Will, it helps separate our identity from the personal self, with its mind, and look to the part of us that generates our thoughts. Meditation is one of its tools. One of the secrets to many forms of meditation is this realization. Most people get frustrated when they start to meditate. Popular techniques are to quiet the mind by counting your breath. Others repeat a mantra silently, a special word or phrase, often in a foreign language. Either is supposed to give clarity to the mind. But what's the first thing that happens? Our mind gets flooded with all sorts of mundane thoughts. Did I pay all my bills? What is on my shopping list? I'm worried about my job. Where will we go for dinner on Saturday? Thoughts like this are normal. Frustration is normal. We think of having no thoughts as the ideal, but an important realization is: "Who is having these thoughts?"

We identify so closely with the mind, with our thoughts, in modern society. We even have the popular phrase, "I think, therefore I am" from philosopher René Descartes, which has become a foundation to modern Western Philosophy. Yet to the philosophers of the hidden arts, both east and west, the "I am" is something beyond thought, beyond our mind. How could "we" fight with the mind, in trying to quiet it, unless the core identity is something other than the mind? True, the mind gives us wonderful blessings and abilities that help shape our identity as human beings and explore our role in the universe, but it is a tool, not an ultimate identity. The true self— what others might call the Soul, Higher Self, Bornless One, or Watcher self —is beyond the mind, and can use the mind like any other tool when we are aligned with our true self. When we are not, and identify mostly with the mind, emotions, or even body, we remain ignorant of the true self, and its potential.

Connection with the true self can come from any of these three forces. Divine Will, Divine Love, and Divine Wisdom lead us all out of the realm of the purely personal into the greater perspective and identity of the true self. One does not need to be a student of Theosophy or any other creed to see their effects. While not everyone experiences them in a lifetime, they are universal to the human experience and are the origin of the best parts of our philosophies, religions, and rituals.

If you are a student of Theosophy and its related lore, one blessing you receive is a worldview that synthesizes many truths into a global perspective. Theosophical lore first took root in 19th Century Europe, bringing the Eastern wisdom of India and Tibet, as well as Egypt and Greece, to a predominantly Christian world. Later material made Christianity more prominent by emphasizing its universal nature for all. The original meaning of the word "catholic," before being associated with a specific church, was "universal." In the end, I think Christ was speaking to everyone in his message of love. Theosophy envisioned a spiritual world where Buddha, Christ, Krishna, Isis, and Orpheus could all be side by side. It wove together our first strands of global mythology and philosophy, reconciling the views of many religions.

Later additions to Theosophical "New Age" lore also brought the wisdom of Jewish Kabalah, alchemy, shamanism, and Paganism. This synthesis would become the foundation of a new way of looking at comparative mythology. Not only could the world's traditions be looked at side by side, but a new body of lore emerged for the modern practitioners who are now exposed to everything, with our mass distribution and electronic communication. It was a wonderful view as we began to develop a global culture, recognizing the truth behind all religions, yet acknowledging and celebrating the diversity of the cultures from which the figures originated.

The inheritors of the Theosophical worldview believed each of the seven colored rays are overseen by a spiritual entity, much like a cosmic manager. These roles were like "offices" and, at different times in our history, different enlightened humans who have moved beyond the personal human realm would occupy the office. It is part of the cycle of human enlightenment and evolution.

It sounds strange to us today, but the idea basically says particularly special people who really mastered one of these divine powers would then become a spiritual beacon, a guide and model to the rest of us struggling with the same experiences. It's similar to the Catholic concept of Saints or the Eastern concept of Bodhisattvas.

Most mystical traditions have their own names for such enlightened people. They are not only inspirations, but allies and guides to the mystics who pray to them and petition for aid. Being human once, they have a greater appreciation for our current situation and lead the way to a more divine perspective. They are icons in the true sense of the word; They illuminate and reveal the spiritual truths by their presence. They are the people who have answered the questions "Who? What? Where? When? Why?" and lived their answers. Many in New Age lore look to the Three Kings of the nativity as such allies.

In the works of Alice Bailey, a former Theosophist who broke from the Theosophical Society to form her own organization, she discussed the "offices" of the rays in detail. Bailey emphasized the office of the Second Ray as the "Planetary Christ." For non-Christians, this can be a hard concept, but basically this figure was a world teacher to disseminate the blessings of Divine Love, what has since become known as "Christ Consciousness" in New Age circles. One who is in "Christ Consciousness" is operating from the perspective of Divine Love, emulating the ideal we have of Jesus Christ. Bailey was a Christian, and while she also had aspects of Eastern lore in her writing, it is not surprising that Christ took more of a dominant role in her own teachings, consciously or unconsciously. Many who aspire to the goal of unconditional love use another name for it, rather than the Christian-centric terms. You can call it anything you want, and many people do.

Bailey's model of the spiritual world included two other roles for the two other primary rays. The Red Ray of Power has the office of the Manu. The name Manu comes from Hindu myth, and is almost the equivalent of the Biblical Adam, the first man in Judeo-Christian mythology. The Hindu Manu is considered a great king, father to all and the one who protected people to survive the Great Flood, somewhat like the Biblical Noah. In Theosophy, the Manu is the archetypal human, a template for human consciousness. In Hebrew mysticism, the archetypal spiritual human is known as the Adam Kadmon.

Many creation myths start out with the first man and first woman. They provide a template for the development of humanity, like the Manu. Each myth looks at it differently, and believes the nature of humanity is slightly different, based upon that tradition's perspective. Judeo-Christian myth has Adam made from clay and Eve made from Adam's rib, giving us a view of the role of the sexes in Judeo-Christian society that influences us, subtly and sometimes not so subtly. In the Norse creation myth, the first couple was Ask and Embla. Ask is the Ash tree while Embla either means Elm tree or perhaps vine, but their names denote humanity's connection to nature and the forest.

The office of the Third Ray is known as the Mahacohen, which roughly translated means "much master" or "great master." This figure is also known as the Lord of Civilization, and oversees the development of human society. While Manu is considered the first king of the world, the Mahacohen is often considered the Secret King of the World. Myths of a secret world leader exist in many traditions, an enlightened king ruling an enlightened nation. Most famous of these are the tales of Shambhala, the secret enlightened city associated with Tibet. Another name for it is Shangri-La. Similar tales of secret kings ruling perfect societies with no crime, no illness and something akin to the Fountain of Youth abound the world over. We could look to the stories of the island nations such as the Celtic Avalon, the Greek islands of Utopia, Hesperides, and Electra, and even fabled lands like Atlantis, Lemuria, and Hybornea as secret nations hidden from humanity. El Dorado is another such myth, from South America. The Christian version of the myth is the Kingdom of Prester John. He was said to rule a mythic perfect Christian nation in the east, and was a descendant of one of the Three Wise Men who visited Jesus at his birth. Those of the Holy Roman Empire, at their highest ideals, aspired to recreate the Kingdom of Prester John in the western world. Many theorize that Shambhala and Prester John's kingdom were one in the same, just put into Christian terms for Christians, and Buddhist terms for Buddhist, but the truth was beyond both. Perhaps they are all the same place, just described by different traditions with different symbols.

Together, the spiritual entities associated with the "offices" of Planetary Christ, Manu and Mahacohen mediate the forces of Divine Love, Divine Will, and Divine Wisdom. Bailey's concepts were much more complicated, including various offices and roles for figures from history, mythology, and religion, but the whole model was formulated around the three rays.

Metaphysical philosophy is always evolving and changing, as we try to describe things that cannot be put into words. My own experience with the three divine forces gave me a new perspective on these forces, and the role models we have to guide us in our understanding of them.

# Chapter Three: A New Vision

My own explorations have given me a great appreciation of a global worldview of spirituality. The more I studied, the more I realized every religion has a valid view of the truth, at least at its core. Sometimes that truth is obscured as the personal views of humanity create dogma, but the original impetus of most spiritual traditions is towards truth, and embodying a valid perspective of the truth. Each has "a" truth, not "the" truth, as any one tradition cannot really claim truth in its entirety.

As a student of comparative mythology, I saw the myths we tell ourselves the world over have similar themes. We express them differently, each culture has its own emphasis on what is important in the story, but they all speak to the human experience. They might answer one of our questions of Who? What? Where? When? And Why? But not all of them are answered all the time. So I kept searching.

My quest took me deeper into the Earth reverent traditions of the western world. While I started my journey after leaving Catholicism exploring eastern religions like Buddhism, Hinduism, Shinto, and Taoism, I ended up looking deeper into the Western mysteries; the Egyptians, Greeks, Romans, Celts, and Norse captured my attention. The mystery schools, secret societies, alchemical laboratories, and the forest groves of the Witch and Druid drew me in. But I never lost my global perspective, still comparing what I learned in the Eastern traditions. Like many of the occultist of the late nineteenth and early twentieth centuries, I not only compared, but also began to synthesize, to create my own worldview.

I began to believe, as many have before me, in the Tradition. Tradition with a capitol "T" that goes beyond all our smaller cultural traditions. The Tradition is the perennial philosophy underlying all world religions and spiritual systems. It is the Tradition rooted in Divine Will, Divine Love and Divine Wisdom, whether individual expressions of it use those words or not. Each religion simply approaches the experience of the Tradition from a different angle, but they are all lead to the same source of Truth.

While leading a meditation group, I had a new vision of the three forces and the figures who guide them in our lives. It was profound and somewhat unsettling, as it didn't exactly fit anything I had read before, yet it made so much sense to me. I asked why, like I always do, and began to do more research, coupled with my own meditations and journaling, to explore the idea I was given.

I began sharing the new vision with others, and got a great response at both the depth and simplicity of it. One of my major problems with a lot of the esoteric and Theosophical lore that has come before is its complexity, bogging down even the simplest concepts making it hard to relate to them.

My second major problem with Theosophy was the emphasis on the Eastern traditions, and, when Western traditions were emphasized, Christianity was favored over other Pagan philosophies. Many occultists at the start of our modern metaphysical movement felt the same, notably author and teacher Dion Fortune. She looked to the Arthurian Mythos, and her own work provided inspiration for my own.

So in vision during a deep meditation, I saw the three colors of the three rays – red to the left of me, with blue to the right. A golden yellow occupied the center. In each color I saw a figure embodying the power of the ray.

Within the central yellow light was a figure like the Dali Lama, which transformed into a more traditional image of the Buddha, from Tibetan tradition rather than the heavy set depictions in Chinese statues. This Buddha was gold and silver, almond faced, with a top knot of braided hair. Eyes were serenely closed and the traditional bindi style marking, a dot at the brow or third eye, was present. Loose clothing was draped across the Buddha, and the left hand was holding a pot of some sort in his lap and the right arm was stretched downward, palm open and extended. He remained sitting in a cross legged lotus position as my gaze shifted to the sides.

In the blue light was first a traditional Mother Mary image from my early Catholic days. Here was the heavenly mother standing, looking down at me, with an outer blue robe and an inner white robe, open veiled and crowned. Her arms were outstretched. As soon as I could acknowledge her, the image morphed into a traditional image of Jesus. It wasn't the gruesome crucified Jesus, but Jesus standing peacefully as the teacher and prophet.

He was in a similar standing pose to Mary, but his hands were turned palms up and his eyes gazing upward. His inner white robe was accented by a robe of red that changed to blue and then red again. Though I know blue eyes are historically unlikely in the person of Jesus, this Christ has the popular artistic depiction of the bearded man with long brown hair and blue eyes. His heart glowed red beneath this robe and seemed to radiate out from the center of this vision to the right of me.

Then I turned to the crimson light to my left, and got a flash of a dark haired, dark robed woman. The meditations I was teaching that day were on the Arthurian Mysteries, so the appearance of the Dali Lama, Buddha, Mary, and Jesus were startling. At last a more familiar and appropriate figure – was it the Lady of the Lake? Vivian? Nimue? Morgan Le Fey perhaps? They are all figures within Arthurian mythology. Then the darkness swirled within the red to reveal the old wizard Merlin.

While most think of Merlin and conjure the image of a blue-cloaked old man with a pointed hat, adorned with yellow moons and stars, the traditional image of Merlin is more of a wild man, or sometimes even a child. The wild man is more akin to a Celtic shaman or Druid – wearing a feathered cloak, animal skins, and looking wild eyed — in the way only a man who has spent a lot of time alone in the forest can look. He is as much prophet wandering the wild as he is civilized magician. There he was with his walking staff and tattered clothes, bathed in the red light.

When I could hold the image of all three figures simultaneously, Buddha, Christ, and Merlin, I received an inner knowing of their significance for me. Like a computer receiving a download of information, all at once these realizations began to hit me, and it took a long while after to process every bit. I'm writing this book in part to not only help me process the information, but to be able to share it in a less dramatic way with others.

Buddhism arose in relationship to the mind. It is a system of practice based on alleviating the suffering caused by the attachments, expectations, and perception of the mind. Wisdom is found by mastering the mind and understanding our perceptions. In many ways, Buddhism distilled the wisdom of Hinduism, as the Hindu tradition has a great understanding and mastery over the forces of consciousness, but Hinduism is so infused with localized customs and culture. Buddhism was a form of wisdom that could be exported from India in a much easier way than classical Hinduism.

Though most Buddhist traditions look at Buddha as an inspiration for the path, and a pioneer, his image in its various forms has become an icon for that form of truth. Obviously it holds an appeal and can work for many, as Buddhism has flourished in various forms wherever it goes. With the Chinese occupation of Tibet, Tibetan Buddhism in particular has come to the forefront of global consciousness and can teach us many things about the mind and perception. While it has many tenets, beliefs and philosophies, it can be seen as based in the wisdom of our Third Ray. Buddha is obviously the icon for this path, and the more terrestrial representative of the Buddhist way is the Tibetan Dali Lama.

Christianity arose after Buddhism, as one took dominance in the West and the other spread throughout the East. At its core, the tenets of Christianity speak of unconditional love. Christ has almost become a synonym for our perception of unconditional, even self-sacrificing, love. After a period of strict patriarchy in Jewish tradition, filled with tribal customs and traditions to keep a people cohesive and strong in a world of persecution and enslavement, they were expecting a political messiah to liberate them. The messiah that appeared was one of philosophy and mysticism, not politics and society.

Though filled with a great many contradictions, Christ's testaments, both officially accepted by the dominant churches and those considered heretical, all speak of love. Christ's message was of loving your neighbor as yourself, and that your heavenly Father loves you. A new compact of redemption was offered. While the blessings of Judaism rarely left the Hebrew tribe, because in many ways the religion, culture, and ethnicity were one, Christianity developed an attitude of accepting all, just as Christ, in his love, shunned none – from king to beggar, fisherman to prostitute. All were loved. Christ embodies, just as Alice Bailey said, the Second Ray of blue light.

Merlin, my figure on the left, was rarely associated with any of these figures. The teachings of Dion Fortune and her own groups equated Merlin as the Manu of the Western world. He embodied that archetypal human figure, a guiding consciousness in the traditions of the Western Mysteries. Not a king himself, his myths are connected with kingship. He is the king-maker. He is in the heart of the Arthurian Mysteries, based upon a time after the rise of Christianity in Europe, all the way to the British Isles, connected to an ancient tradition that stretches before the times of Christianity and even Buddhism, more akin to the oldest tribes of the Stone Age people who built the standing stone monuments prior to the Celtic invasions. Merlin is a wizard, magician, Druid, Witch, and foremost, shaman.

His role in this triad was to represent the Divine Will, what must be done, which is the hallmark of many magical traditions. All magicians use their will to move the forces of the universe, to make magic. His presence in our triad restores not only the indigenous European traditions, the old Pagan wisdom, but forges a link to the indigenous tribal customs across the world. The mysteries of magic, of will, in Europe are the same as those in the Americas, Africa, Asia, and Australia. While based in British folklore, he is a universal force now recognized the world over. He doesn't have the same religious institutions as Buddha and Christ, but he tends to be just as popular in media, starting with the Medieval Arthurian romance cycles all the way to printed books, movies, comics, toys, and musicals. When we look at the archetype of Merlin, we see him as Gandalf the wizard in *Lord of the Rings*, *Harry Potter*'s Dumbledore, and even *Star Wars'* Obi Wan Kenobi and Yoda. What he lacks in institutional power, he makes up for in capturing our popular consciousness since his name was first used in the British myth cycles.

Without realizing it at the time, I found my three wise men. Here were three wise men for this age, each all "speaking" to and for people who are living in the world today. As citizens of the new global village, we are all probably at least passingly familiar with all three. Each has a link to the past, yet are part of our present and most likely to influence our future. We know of them, their lives, their actions, their background, be it fact or myth. They can guide us in ways the largely anonymous wise men of the previous ages cannot. They each have far more lore than our Three Kings.

Are these the only wise men of our age? No, of course not. Many religious traditions carry their own wise men. I could have just as easily had a vision of three other figures equally worthy of praise. I could look to Moses, Mohamed, Quetzalcoatl, Lao Tzu, John Dee, or Aleister Crowley. But these were the ones who appeared to me.

Where are the wise women? There are many, some of whom are interwoven into the history and myth of these figures – Quan Yin, Mother Mary, Mary Magdalane, Vivian, Nimue, and Morgana Le Fey. A few played a role in my own vision. Yet these three male figures are the ones we most easily recognize. Perhaps that will change in time. Coming from a Goddess reverent tradition myself, I do hope the divine feminine will be more actively pursued, and I'll be sharing the influence of women upon these three men, but these men are the figures that appeared most prominently in my own vision and the information about that is what I feel compelled to share at this time.

While I truly appreciate each of these men, none of them are perfect. None of them got it entirely "right" completely, whatever "right" might be. Each focused on a specific perspective of what they felt was important, and a segment of our population followed suit. They each answered the questions of "Who? What? Where? When? And Why?" to the best of their ability and shared what they learned with them, to help others answer these questions.

Collectively however, they provide a more complete picture through the lens of Divine Will, Divine Love and Divine Wisdom, than any of them create on their own. For a more complete picture could we look at four traditions? Five? Ten? Yes, but the model of the three rays gives us a balanced view without getting overly complicated. Many of the founders of spiritual groups and organizations in the twentieth century used the model of three root traditions to provide balance and perspective. Dion Fortune was herself a student of esoteric Christianity, Hermetic magic, and the nature based traditions embodied in the Arthurian myths. The three provide a balanced perspective.

Each of the three philosophies of Buddha, Christ, and Merlin, has strengths and weakness. By looking at them collectively and synthesizing a combination that speaks to us and our needs, and as a global society, we can come ever closer to the Truth with a capitol "T" without dogmatically confusing our view of Truth as the truth for all. The universal Tradition is the only keeper of Truth; we all approach it through our various earthy traditions and combinations of philosophy and practice.

The ability to function both collectively and individually at the same time is the hallmark of our newly developing age. To do so, we need to seek out the Truth for ourselves, yet apply what we learn to the betterment of ourselves, our societies, and the world at large. We must be healers and transformers of ourselves, our people, and the planet, and we must encourage the freedom for everyone else to do the same.

# Chapter Four: The Way of the Buddha

The story of Buddha was originally preserved in the oral tradition of early Buddhists in the sixth century B.C. His followers summarized his life, teachings and messages, and passed this information on to new students. The teachings were not formally committed to writing until four hundred years later, in what are considered the earliest Buddhist texts. While at first scholars assumed the story of Buddha's life as presented in these texts was a factual account of his journey, now most scholars of Buddhism believe the first Buddhists, as ancient Indians, were less concerned about factual chronology and more about preserving the teachings and philosophy of Buddha, which now had been more clearly divided and codified into separate sections. There was likely a period in the strict oral tradition where the accounts of Buddha's life were adapted, simplified, or even exaggerated to fit the standard of the philosophy and practice of what Buddhism was becoming.

Like most religious founders and leaders, we might never know the true details of the historical Buddha's life, but the story passed on in the Buddhist tradition is really more important than any lost biographical details. The story gives us a way to understand the teaching of the Buddha in the context of human life.

*The man who would become Buddha was born in Limbini, a prince of the land of Kapilavastu on the border of India and Nepal. His father, King Sudhodana, ruled the Sakya, a clan of warriors. On the night when Gautama Buddha was conceived, his mother, Queen Maya, dreamt that a white elephant with not two, but six white tusks, had entered her right side. This dream was an omen that the Buddha, the universal emperor, was to be her son. She left her kingdom to have her child in her father's kingdom, but gave birth to him while on the road, passing through the village of Limbini. It is said that immediately he was able to walk and speak without effort. The baby was given the name Siddhartha, which means "he who achieves his aim."*

*Siddhartha was soon visited by the holy man and ascetic known as Asita, who came down from his Himalayan home upon hearing of the child's birth and* the subsequent celebrations. Asita had been the tutor to the King. As the King presented his son, Siddhartha's feet turned and rested upon the head of Asita. Asita watched the birthmarks on the child's feet and predicted that either he would be a great king or a great holy man. Asita was both joyful and sad. He was joyful for such a great man to be born into the world, but sad he would not be able to study under this potential Buddha, as he would die before the Buddha's teaching could begin.

Seven days after his birth, Queen Maya died and her sister Maha Pajapati, took her place in caring for young Siddhartha. The young prince was raised in opulence, having three palaces just for himself to occupy seasonally. He had all of his desires satisfied and there was no expense too great for him.

At age twelve, Siddhartha was visited by the Brahmans, the wise men of the land. Seven out of the eight Brahmans predicted the destiny of this child to either be a great king and leader, or a great holy man. Only one predicted unequivocally that Siddhartha would be the Buddha. The wise men said he would devote himself to asceticism if he cast his eyes upon age, sickness, or death, and if he was to meet a hermit.

King Sudhodana did not want his son to grow up to be an ascetic holy man, so he shielded him from all religious teachings and people. He proclaimed the words death and grief were forbidden, never to be spoken to his son. At age sixteen, Sudhodana arranged Siddhartha's marriage to the beautiful princess Yasodhara, a cousin. After their wedding she gave birth to a son, Rahula. For the first twenty nine years of the Prince's life, he had everything he could need in his sheltered world, but he soon realized material wealth was not the secret to life and became restless.

One day Siddhartha decided to visit his subjects. If he was to be great king, he would need to know his people. Deciding to visit a nearby town, his father had arranged for everything to be cleared, cleansed, and made beautiful. Anything sad or ugly in the village needed to be removed. But the old king's efforts were in vain. As he traveled through the streets of the village, Siddhartha saw an elderly man, wrinkled and hunched over. The prince was disturbed by this. Up to this point, he had never seen an elder. His charioteer, Channa, told him that was the fate of all who lived, to grow old. He was astonished. No one prepared him for this sad fact. As he continued his journey through the village *he met a man who was ill with an incurable disease. His illness crippled him and left him invalid. The prince was likewise shocked, never really knowing disease. As the journey continued Siddhartha spied a funeral procession and saw the corpse being carried and was horrified. He had never contemplated death before. Lastly, before leaving the village, he saw a beggar, a self- chosen ascetic, who told the prince that he had chosen to leave the world, to find peace through balance without suffering or joy.*

*From that moment on, Siddhartha decided to abandon his life and become an ascetic. He went to his father, asking permission to leave the palace, family, and his royal life to become an ascetic. His father was struck with grief at the idea of losing his son and placed guards around the walls to prevent him from leaving, as well as increasing his pleasure, entertainment and distractions within the palace. While he loved his wife and son, Siddhartha realized the impermanence of life and the vanity of desire.*

*With the aid of Channa, he mounted his horse Kantaka and rode out of the city gates. It is said the gods muffled the horses hooves so he could escape without the guards, or his father's, notice. Siddhartha gave up all his possession, his horse and his robe, and cut off his hair. He began his ascetic life, begging for alms in another kingdom. He was recognized by the king of the land, Magadha, and when the king heard of his quest, he offered his kingdom to this wise beggar. Siddhartha refused and continued his quest.*

*Siddhartha found two teachers, and followed each for a time. He became the monk Gautama, a family name, and was accepted as a disciple. He learned their doctrines and excelled at their practices, so much so, that each master asked him to continue the lineage. Their teaching did not lead to true peace, and he, along with five other disciples, left to practice more extreme forms of asceticism. For five years, he gave up all worldly goods, restricting his diet to a nut a day and practicing self-mortification. While bathing in a stream he collapsed and almost drowned. He realized this path failed to give him the insight he needed and rejected its dangerous practices.*

*He accepted milk and rice pudding from a local village girl and realized there must be a Middle Way between indulgence and mortification. He traveled to a deer park at Isipatana, near what is Benares today. Siddhartha found a sacred Bodhi tree, and swore to sit beneath it and not leave until he found the wisdom he sought. His five companions thought he had become lazy, and left him.*

*The demon Mara did not want Gautama to attain enlightenment, so he sent his three beautiful daughters to distract him. Gautama would not be distracted. Mara then sent an army of demons to destroy the future Buddha. Gautama was unmoved. Finally Mara came at him personally with a great blade that could cleave mountains, but Gautama remained undisturbed. He sat under the Bodhi tree with his left hand in his lap, and his right hand over his right knee, fingertips touching the earth, so the Earth was a witness to the defeat of Mara. The demon was forced to leave, unsuccessful in his attempt to destroy, or even distract, Gautama.*

*Here, after forty-nine days, in the fifth lunar month, under the Bodhi tree at the age of thirty-five, the former prince Siddhartha attained enlightenment, gaining knowledge of how things really are and earned the title of Buddha, meaning "awakened one." He learned the source of suffering is ignorance, and the means by which to resolve it.*

*First he perceived in meditation all of his previous incarnations and understood the karma, or cause and effect, of his actions.*

*In the second awareness, he saw the death and rebirth of all beings and understood the cycle of life and death.*

*For his third realization, he perceived the Four Noble Truths. He then perceived the Noble Eightfold Path and ultimately attained the nine virtues. He understood that every being in the universe posseses the potential to be a future buddha.*

*The Buddha could have entered Nirvana, the state of supreme liberation, or he could teach his realizations to the world. He feared the world was not ready for his teaching, the dharma. A Brahmin asked him to stay and begged him to teach the law. He was convinced that some would be ready for the teaching and understand.*

*His first converts were the five ascetic companions he had when he was living in the wild. He preached to them his first sermon in the deer park at Benares and outlined his principles. The community grew in size, and came to include his son and cousin, and eventually allowed women through persuasion of his step-mother and his cousin. He founded his Buddhist community of monks* and nuns and began traveling the Ganges plain teaching for the next forty-five years.

After hearing about Siddhartha's enlightenment, King Sudhodana dispatched messengers and delegations to invite the former prince back home. Each delegation, nine in all, became converts and, dismissing worldly matters, forgot to give Buddha the message from his father. Only the tenth delegation, led by a childhood friend of Siddhartha's, was able to deliver the message before becoming a converts. Since rainy season was over, Buddha agreed to travel, and preached along the way. Once back in Kapilavastu, a midday meal was prepared for Buddha and his followers, but the king gave no special invitation. Buddha begged for alms midday, angering the King.

He told Buddha, "Ours is a warrior lineage. None of us have begged for alms."

Buddha responded with, "It is not the custom of your royal lineage. But it is the custom of my Buddha lineage. Thousands of Buddhas have begged for alms."

Buddha and his followers returned to the palace for a meal and a dharma talk. On the visit many of the royal family ended up converting to Buddhism. His cousin Devadatta became a monk, but later rejected Buddha's teaching, became an enemy, and tried to kill his cousin several times without success. Upon Sudhodana's deathbed, Buddha returned, preached the Dharma and Sudhodana become a convert before his death.

At age eighty, Buddha became very sick. He journeyed northwards to the river Hiranyavati. He ate the food offered to him by a blacksmith. He came to the river and took a bath and made a bed of the trees. In a reclining pose with his right hand supporting his head and his left on his body, he prepared for death. He met with one last visitor, a scholar who became his last disciple. Before he passed, he exhorted to his followers, "All creations are impermanent. Diligently work towards your own liberation." Buddha taught that no one would succeed him as leader other than the teachings. The doctrine would be the master of the lineage. He entered into deep meditation, passing through the various levels of ecstasy and passed into Nirvana, beyond rebirth in this or any unseen world. Buddha was said to pass on the Full moon, in the month of May, known in the Indian calendar as Wesak, which is still celebrated as a holiday among Buddhists and mystics. The Buddha's earthly body was cremated.

The life of Buddha is really a story about the life of duty, not the duty of perceived expectations from family and society, but the duty we each have to follow the dictates of our own soul. Despite difficulties, uncertainty, and many easier opportunities, Buddha followed the path he was called to, and through that exploration, found wisdom. By sharing that wisdom, he founded a tradition.

Buddha means "the awakened one". In realizing the suffering and attachment in the perspective most people call "normal" consciousness, he has awoken out of it, as if it were a bad dream. In this new awakened state, he can see clearly, and the newfound wisdom sprang from an awakened, or enlightened, wisdom rather than the half-truths of a sleeping consciousness, lacking perspective on the true nature of reality.

While to the Buddhist this perspective portrays the true nature of reality, from my own perspective it is just one third of the worldview, just as Christianity or Paganism does not paint a completely accurate picture. Multiple views gives us a greater understanding of the complexity of the world and the human condition.

The story of Buddha is meant to express the lessons he discovered in the basic order in which he discovered them, helping the aspiring Buddhist identify with shock, struggle, and suffering, and leading to similar conclusions about detachment and balance.

Buddha is born, like many religious figures, to royalty. At first that would seemingly separate him from everyday man, yet in many tales of royal heroes and prophets, the framework of royalty reminds us that we are all royalty in the sense we all have divine origin. We all have something that makes us special.

In Hinduism, Buddha's royalty is considered god-like, for he is recognized as the ninth avatar of the god Vishnu. Vishnu is the dissolver, one third of a cosmic trinity with Brahma and Shiva. In the Hindu tradition, gods take on various incarnations as fully realized beings, to bring their wisdom to the world and remind humanity of how to live in balance and harmony. While avatars are remarkable individuals who are born already aware of their divine nature, we are all aspects of the divine, an Atman god self, incarnate in the world. We simply have to journey to realize this true nature.

Early in his life Buddha experiences his first loss, though it is not emphasized in the tale, the lost of his mother Queen Maya. This is the first attachment to be released, though she is immediately replaced by a substitute mother figure. Although Maha Pajapati is greatly honored and loved Siddhartha very much, there is something to be said about the loss of the original mother. It seems like the focus of support comes from the father, and the father's best ability is to provide materially for young Siddhartha, making sure he wants for nothing. While enjoying a life of riches, he is bereft of the spiritual and emotional support his mother could have provided. With empty materialism, he seeks out a new path. "When" does he begin his quest? He hears the call of spirit upon realization of the existence of suffering.

On his journey out of the kingdom, Siddhartha faced realizations that all of us have to face eventually about the nature of human life. Perhaps he faced them later in life than most and that caused both his great turmoil and his quest for awakening. He saw the faces of old age, illness, and death. All that grows in the world will eventually die. Nothing is permanent in the world of form. As all things can grow strong, all things are susceptible to damage and decay. To believe otherwise is foolish and a wise man accepts this is the way of the body.

His fourth vision—of an ascetic—seemed to be the key out of this misery and suffering. By renouncing the world, and placing emphasis on the spiritual, rather than the material with its attachment and cravings, the source of suffering can be stilled.

In his quest to truly understand, he went to extremes until he found a Middle Way. He doesn't know "how" to complete his quest, so he tries everything with diligence, until settling on the path between extremes. Through simple meditation beneath the Bodhi Tree, unmoved by challenge or distraction, he found the way things truly were and awakened. Most importantly, Buddha realized his new-found condition of awakening was not unique. All beings in the universe have this potential. All seek to become Buddhas. He was not the only one. Yet his identity, answering the question "who am I?" is the Buddha, his vision of his true state of being.

While Buddha attained knowledge of the true nature of the world, he could have left the world completely, and merged with the spiritual bliss of Nirvana. Yet he didn't. He chose to put his knowledge into action, thereby finding divine wisdom. What is wisdom but the use of knowledge? Anyone can learn anything, but the importance is in what you do with that knowledge. How does it aid you, others, and the world? He chose to stay and to not only teach the intellectual outline of his tradition, summed up in the Four Noble Truths and the Eightfold Path , but to model the result of these teachings, and live with them in the world of form everyday. Buddha thereby answers the question of "what?" and more specifically, "what am I to do?" or "what is my purpose?" His purpose is to share the dharma, his teachings of right action.

From his new point of realization, he dealt with his past, including his father who tried to keep him from the life of a holy man. He dealt with his entire family, including the seeming enemy in his cousin, Devadatta, who tried to kill him. He modeled his teachings of non-attachment in the face of such difficulties. He dealt with perceived sexism, and the role of women in the new Buddhist movement. He faced death through sickness, before merging with Nirvana. All are very human experiences for one viewed by many as godlike. He brought his divinity, the wisdom from his awakening, into all of his relationships, old and new. "Why" does he do it? He does so in order to liberate everyone, as he was liberated.

It would have been far easier for the Buddha to say give up your desires and attachments and then leave the world of flesh and form, but it was far more important for him to stay and show people *how* to do so. He answers the "where" of his life by staying in the world, and specifically near the areas where he was raised, traveling India and the outlying regions, giving roots to his tradition and building communities of Buddhists who supported each other on the path. The teachings are not divinely transmitted, though esoteric schools of Buddhism certainly have mystical techniques and initiations. The essence of Buddhist practice is guidance from the teachings of the Buddha, ultimately having your own awakening to divine wisdom, and living from that newly awakened state.

# Chapter Five: The Journey of Christ

The primary source of information on the life of Jesus Christ is the four canonical Gospels of Matthew, Mark, Luke, and John. While they share similarities in terms of the life and mission of Jesus, with Matthew, Mark, and Luke being more similar than the Gospel of John, they also have some variations and contradictions, so there is no one absolute version of the journey of Christ. Each one paints a different portrait of the man known today as Jesus Christ.

There are also a wide range of unofficial Gospels dating from roughly the same time period with even more divergent interpretations. While they were all a part of the early Christian tradition, the Catholic Church later officially recognized these four Gospels as "cannon" and considers all others as heretical.

Most modern Christians, unaccustomed to reading the Gospels as a single story, but rather in short passages, have mentally collected the four into one composite tale that isn't true to any of the Gospels, but has become the "fifth" Gospel. Some include details from the unofficial "Gnostic" Gospels too, such as the Gospel of Thomas or the Gospel of Philip. This is the collective image most hold of Jesus, allowing a wide range of personal interpretation of his message, actions, motives, and reasons.

Modern mystics typically divorce Christ from the various dogmas of the Christian Churches, and look at him as a spiritual teacher. By word and deed, they seek out his message. They do not look at the theological questions of his messianic qualities, and the debates about sin and salvation, but see Christ much more like the eastern traditions see the embodied gurus and avatars. These beings are divine spiritual masters in the flesh, walking upon the Earth.

In the case of the enlightened gurus, they are normal humans who attain enlightenment and mastery in this lifetime. In the case of avatars, they are aspects of deity that incarnate in the world to bring a new message, such as the Hindu Krishna, an avatar of the god Vishnu.

When approached in such a manner, the story of Jesus Christ becomes much more helpful in understanding the force of Divine Love.

*An angel of the lord, Archangel Gabriel the messenger, visited Mary, a young Jewish woman living in Galilee of Nazareth. Though Mary was engaged to marry Joseph, a carpenter, the angel told her she would conceive a son by the power of the Holy Spirit. She would still marry Joseph, carry the child to term and upon his birth name him Jesus. Mary couldn't believe the angel's words, for she was a virgin, but the angel told her this child would be the Lord's own son, and that "nothing is impossible with God." Mary believed the words of the angel and rejoiced in her love and devotion to God.*

*Just as the angel foretold, Mary miraculously became pregnant through the Holy Spirit. Mary told Joseph of her pregnancy and the angel's message. At first Joseph was understandably upset and wanted to break their engagement, but he treated Mary kindly, and the Lord sent an angel to Joseph in his dreams to confirm Mary's story, and to make clear that this birth, and Joseph's marriage to Mary, was God's will.*

*During this time, Caesar Augustus decreed that a census be taken of the Roman world, including Judea. Everyone in the empire had to go to their home town to register in the census. Joseph came from the line of David, and was required to go back to the town of Bethlehem to register. Because of all the travel, the inn at Bethlehem was too crowded, and Joseph and Mary were forced to stay in a stable for shelter. Mary gave birth to Jesus in the stable, wrapped him in cloth and placed him in the manger. An angel of the Lord appeared to the local shepherds that night, and announced the messiah had been born in the Town of David. The shepherds went Bethlehem to see the Christ child. There they found Jesus, Mary, and Joseph, and after their visit, spread the word about this child and the angel's message.*

*Before Jesus was born, three Wise Men, three kings and magicians from the east, saw the star that signified the birth of a wondrous child. They met with King Herod, ruler of Judea while looking for the child who would be King of the Jews. Herod told the Wise Men to report back to him when they found the child, for he too, wanted to worship and honor the Christ child. He secretly plotted to kill the child but obviously didn't tell the wise men his plan. They continued to follow the Star of Bethlehem until they found the child and his parents. Most art* depicts the kings in the stable with Jesus, but more likely they found him years after his birth. They honored him with gifts of gold, frankincense, and myrrh. The wise men were warned by God in a dream that Herod wanted to destroy the child, so they did not report back to the King of Judea when they left. So Herod ordered the death of all young male children in Bethlehem, hoping to execute Jesus, and prevent himself from losing Judea to this new prophecized "King of the Jews." Jesus was not among those killed, and escaped with his parents. Mostly likely he escaped to Egypt, only to return to Nazareth years later.

*Figure 1: Star of Bethlehem*

The early life of Jesus is shrouded in mystery. Most believe he lived a fairly ordinary life, despite his heritage. He learned his father's trade as a carpenter. Others believe Mary and Joseph were secretly part of an esoteric Jewish tradition known as the Essenes. Mary was prepared for her role as the mother of the Christ and Jesus was trained in their mysticism from an early age. His training *might have potentially included travel to the mystery schools of Egypt, which would have been fairly accessible to his family at the time, or as far as the British Isles to train with the Celtic priests known as the Druids, or to India to study with the Brahmins.*

*Jesus begins his public ministry through a baptism by John. Known as John the Baptist, and reportedly a cousin of Jesus', he immersed followers in a flowing river to cleanse them of their sin. Gnostic mystics believe that John the Baptist was the reincarnation of the Old Testament prophet Elijah, whose return would precede the coming of the Messiah. John himself foretold the coming of someone greater than he, a messiah as well. Jesus came from Galilee to be baptized by John, even though most Christians believe Jesus to be without sin. The ritual brought him into deeper contact with the Holy Spirit and a heavenly voice revealed to Jesus his own mission on Earth.*

*The voice of the Holy Spirit led Jesus into the desert. There he wandered, fasting for forty days and forty nights. Satan came to him, tempting him. While many popular theologies describe Satan as the source of evil, this "adversary" is really more akin to a tester, using temptation and adversity to test the faith of humanity. Satan revealed Jesus could use his powers to create miracles, such as transforming stones into loaves of bread. He also offered Jesus control of all the kingdoms of the world, in return for worshiping Satan. Jesus refused all of these temptations, and when Satan was defeated, angels brought manna to nourish him and his trial was over.*

*Jesus traveled widely, first going to the Sea of Galilee. There he took on twelve disciples to aid him in his work, recruiting some from the fishermen there on the sea. The disciples included Peter, Andrew, James, John, Phillip, Bartholomew, Matthew, Thomas, James son of Alphaeus, Thaddeus, Simon, and Judas. They consisted of his inner circle, and the gathering of twelve was a reference to the twelve tribes of Israel. It is also reminiscent of a coven, traditionally with twelve members and a thirteenth as leader.*

*Mary Magdalene was also a prominent and controversial follower of Jesus, starting with him in his early ministry and following him until the end. Orthodox interpretations show her as a redeemed prostitute and a minor figure in the early Christian movement. Mystics see her as a full disciple and akin to a priestess to Christ. Some have even suggested that Jesus was not celibate, but*

*Buddha, Christ, Merlin*

Mary Magdalene was his wife and potentially bore him children. Jesus' ministry attracted not only religious men, but women, children – people from all backgrounds.

Jesus spoke simply to the people who came to listen to him preach. He taught in parables, metaphors and stories, relating the wisdom he held to common symbols and experiences people could understand. He simplified many of the complex and archaic traditions of the time, where people were more concerned about the details of the law, rather than its spirit and intention. While Jesus and his followers felt they were totally in alignment with the spirit of the traditions before them in Judaism, many traditional Jews saw them as heretics.

The main principles in the teachings of Christ were to love God with your entire heart, soul, mind, and strength; to love your neighbor as you would love yourself and the power of forgiveness to heal and redeem.

Jesus performed many amazing feats. Some would call them miracles. Others attribute them to knowledge of medicine and herbalism. Still others would describe them as magic, for magic can encompass both.

Wherever he traveled, people would bring the sick and crippled to Jesus, to be cured of all illness and disease. Sometimes he simply spoke to the person, touched the ill or used simple material components, like mud and spit, to effect a cure. Jesus cured lepers, the blind, the lame, the paralyzed, and infirm. He also cured people by exorcising demons that had possessed them.

Jesus performed miracles with the forces of nature. He demonstrated the ability to walk on water. He transformed water into wine at a wedding reception. He multiplied a few loaves and fishes into enough to feed a large group of people. He controlled a storm and cursed a fig tree to wither. He even resurrected a dead man, Lazarus.

This new ministry got the attention of the authorities. While traditional Jews founds his practices heretical, they wanted to have the Romans deal with him.

The priests sought to arrest Jesus quietly, not in front of the crowds of his followers, as they feared a riot. So the apostle Judas betrayed him, indicating who Jesus was to the soldiers by kissing Jesus after the Last Supper Feast.

At the Last Supper with the apostles, Jesus taught them of the Eucharist, taking the bread and saying "this is my body" and taking the wine and saying *"this is my blood." While paralleling the sacred feast of many Pagan agricultural traditions, this established a ritual to be the foundation of the Christian movement after Jesus' death. He was then taken away by the soldiers to await crucifixion. Judas was given thirty pieces of silver for his betrayal, but he was overwhelmed with guilt and hung himself.*

*The priests had the soldiers bring Jesus before Roman authorities hoping to incite Roman fear that Jesus, being proclaimed as messiah, or King of the Jews, was a threat to Roman law, and that he encouraged his followers not to pay taxes to the Romans. The Roman governor of Judea, Ponticus Pilate, did not find Jesus guilty of any capitol offense, but sent him back to King Herod Antipas, son of Herod the Great. Herod Antipas already had John the Baptist killed. Herod sent Jesus back to Pilate, who was forced to execute Jesus because of the gathering Jewish crowds demanding his death for claiming the title King of the Jews. Pilate asked Jesus if he was the King of the Jews, to which Jesus responded, "So you say."*

*After being condemned, Jesus was flogged and beaten by the soldiers, and a crown of thorns placed upon his head. He was brought to Golgotha, a hill outside of Jerusalem. There he was brutally crucified, nailed onto a wooden cross that he was forced to carry himself, flanked by two criminals who were similarly executed. He said, "Father, into your hands I commit my spirit." The sky turned dark for three hours. A Roman solider named Longinus later pierced his side with a spear.*

*Upon Jesus' death, his body was given to Mary Magdalene, Joseph of Arimathea, and his followers. Jesus' body was cleaned and given proper burial, entombed within a cave. On the third day, the women returned to the tomb to find the stone covering moved and the tomb empty. Jesus had risen and appeared to many of his followers before he ascended bodily into heaven as the resurrected Christ. Later the Holy Spirit descended upon the apostles on the day of Pentecost, as tongues of flame. With the flames upon them, they could speak with the voice of the Holy Spirit. The apostles went on to form the basis of what we know as Christianity, for Christ never used that term. Their teachings, or at least the writings attributed to them and the early Christians who heard them speak, became the Gospels, the New Testament forming the scriptural foundation for Christianity.*

There are many themes and interpretations to the story of Jesus. So many, in fact, that a wide range of Christian denominations have popped up over the centuries, each espousing a unique view of the Christ. It's interesting that a story essentially about love and sacrifice, can create such division contrary to Christ's own message.

Christ literally means "anointed one" and a direct translation of the title would be "covered in oil." Yet the term means so much more. One who is anointed with sacred oils and perfumes is considered holy and being prepared for something. Initiates of the Mystery Traditions across the world are anointed with sacred oils before undergoing initiation.

The word Christ has been translated from the Hebrew word meaning Messiah, and in such traditions, Messiah refers to the future anointed King, who will liberate the Hebrew people from captivity, and usher in a golden age of peace. Most envisioned such a Messiah to be a political or military leader in uniting the tribes, as well as a spiritual leader. The vision of Jesus as messiah did not fit most people's expectations. Ironically, most major Christian movements envision a second coming of Christ, which will usher in the end of the world and a golden age for believers, much more in line with the Jewish concept of the Messiah. Jesus answered the question of "who" he is and would be by redefining the concept of Messiah as his spiritual mission. He had to be true to himself, to his relationship with God the Father, and not simply fulfill the wishes of the masses and the expected role of the Messiah.

When we look to the words and actions of Jesus as a Christ figure, divorced from the theology, politics and dogma that followed him, we have a somewhat different vision. Mystics who look at the universality of spiritual experience see a very different Jesus than most Christians, and see a different purpose to Christianity than the mainstream churches.

To be Christian means to be "Christ-like." Christians aspire to be what they envision Christ to be. Yet many believe to be Christian simply means to have faith and believe in Christ as the messiah, or to follow the religion created after his death. The true meaning of Christianity is to be Christ-like in thought, word, and deed.

Jesus respected some of the traditions of the past, but did not cling to the Torah, the Old Testament, for absolute guidance. The older traditions that did not work in his day he rejected, and simplified his message to two easy words: love and forgiveness. Specific rules mattered less if you were living in a state of love and forgiveness. In many ways, Jesus' teachings were really counter-culture – then and even now. He understood "what" his purpose was, to model love and forgiveness, even in the face of the most heinous acts of barbarism, death by crucifixion.

To the mystic, Jesus' story is the story of any initiate devoted to love. His birth is similar to many extraordinary spiritual seekers, in the sense that it is unusual. Many mystics and prophets have unusual signs and omens surrounding their birth. It heralds a potential shift in the energies of the world, and the universe responds, and those wise enough to see the response know something new is being brought to human consciousness. While the "when" of his birth is signaled by the star, he hears the internal call to start his ministry at his thirtieth year. He is recognized by John the Baptist, tested by Satan in a personal trial of sorts and is then ready to do his work in the world, much like testing in school or a trade. In astrological terms, twenty-nine and a half is the end of the first Saturn cycle, when you are considered "cosmically" an adult in the world and aware of your true responsibilities.

One of the constant and from the mystic's point of view misunderstood themes to Christ's life is his dual nature. He is human, but also depicted as divine, as the "son of God." He is born of earthly mother and divine father. This theme is repeated in world mythologies, most notably in the story of Hercules, the demigod of mortal mother and divine father in the sky god Zeus, and even Merlin, son of a mortal woman and a spirit or demon. When asked if he is the Messiah, Son of God, or King of the Jews, he responds with, "So you say." Jesus defines who he is, and doesn't concern himself with how others define him. He stays true to his spiritual vision of the messiah, rather than debate the political expectations of the messiah from both the Jewish people and the Romans.

Mystics believe his nature is actually shared by everybody. We are all mortal. We are all divine. We are all capable of achieving Christ's level of consciousness. His whole ministry was about empowering us all through love and forgiveness. In John 14:12, he says, "Verily, verily, I say unto you, He that believeth in me, the works that I do shall he do also; and greater works than these shall he do; because I go unto my Father." The passage is interpreted in many ways, but one of the most empowering is that we shall become "Christ-like" and capable of miracles through the principles espoused by Jesus in his ministry.

Today it is called "Christ Consciousness" and embodies the second of the three rays of Theosophical thought. From this perspective, Jesus was a type of holy magician. His miracles are a form of magic. While many are done seemingly spontaneously, others use material components, like a sorcerer's spell, such as mud and spit. He transformed or multiplied objects, rather than conjuring them from thin air. When his later apostles went forth and performed miracles, they were seen as on par with other magicians of their day with whom they were in competition, such as Simon Magus. Considered a heretic by Christians, Simon Magus' work was not all that different from the apostles, even though he was not Christian.

The secret of Christ's magic is through his loving connection with the Divine and all of creation. Through love he understood the inherent connection of all people and things with God. His message was about union with the Divine as embodied by the Holy Father. His magic and healing worked through that connection of unconditional love. When you truly understand and operate from the perspective that all things are connected through love, you can create change through that love. Though his message of love is universal, Jesus planted it in the fertile soil of Judaism. He chose the "where" of his ministry wisely, incarnating in an area of the world known for its religious intensity, even today. From those roots, it spread through the Roman Empire and to the world.

According to Christian theology, God so loved the world that he gave his son to redeem the world from sin. Jesus so loved the world that he laid down his life to redeem everyone. While I'm not so sure I personally agree with the concept of martyrdom and sacrifice as part of the mystic's path, I do see the story of Jesus as the wise man of true and unconditional love. His love is the answer to the question of "why" he performed his ministry and modeled this new level of consciousness.

# Chapter Six: The Mission of Merlin

Was Merlin real? It's a question I've asked myself many times. Most people unfamiliar with the British folklore would either assume the starry-robed magician with the conical hat is absolute fact, as many believe all the old romances of King Arthur and Camelot to be history, not mythology, or conversely believe the stories of the Round Table, knights, and Merlin to be entire fabrications, without any factual basis. Neither is the absolute truth.

Merlin is actually mentioned in the historic records of Britain. But this Merlin is not so familiar to modern people, and the history he appears in is often suspect. It's not really clear if he is a figure of legend that ended up in the historic narratives of England, or a historic figure that has be reinvented so many times that he has grown into a myth.

The first historic reference to Merlin is found in a text called *Y Gododdin.* This brief mention has "Mirdyn" as a warrior. Myrddin later became the popular Welsh spelling, and was modernized to the more familiar Merlin. Several later references put him in the realm of bards, closer to the Celtic magicians of his day. Poems and prophecies were attributed to him. This Merlin is considered a madman, poet, and prophet, living wild in the forest. Merlin's most famous early references is the work of Geoffrey of Monmouth, the *History of the Kings of Britain.* Geoffrey takes this Merlin figure from folklore, and weaves him into our now more familiar history of King Arthur, though Merlin's role is greatly diminished compared to the story familiar to us today. Merlin actually exits the story well before the rise of Arthur and is not present in Camelot. But Geoffrey's material forms the foundation of the popular Arthurian romances we know today through books, movies and television.

Geoffrey created two important documents, *The Prophecies of Merlin* and the *The Life of Merlin,* to follow *The History of the Kings of Britain.* They portray the Merlin of folk-history as a prophetic child who goes on to become the mad man of the forest. Geoffrey claimed to be getting his information on Merlin, Arthur and the other kings and knights, from an older historical record that he adapted and modernized for the people of his time.

If this Merlin was actually drawn from history, it is more likely Geoffrey's story was based upon two historic Merlins, not one. The two Merlins have become known as Merlin Ambrosius, a name associated with a Romano-British war leader, and Merlinus Caledonensis, the wild man of the northern forest.

They are not the only two figures associated with Merlin. In fact, many students of magic and the esoteric arts believe that there have been many Merlins throughout history. "Merlin" is more of a title or office. Different people in each age occupy the office of the Merlin, envisioned by some as High Priest and Chief Magician of Britain.

Occultists like Dion Fortune considered Merlin to be the Manu, the archetypal man, of the western world, coming from the fabled land of Atlantis. He brought with him the art and science of sacred kingship, helping bring the land in harmony with its people. Failure to have this partnership with the planet, and the abuses of its power, was one of the reasons for the fall of Atlantis. The Atlantis story's lessons are as appropriate for us as they were to the ancient Greeks when Plato first wrote about the island nation in the west.

Merlin was seen by the magicians of the early twentieth century as a pure consciousness that could be expressed by particularly noteworthy individuals full of magical inspiration. Modern magicians have associated this consciousness with historic figures such as St. Francis of Assisi, Roger Bacon, John Dee, and Reverend Kirk.

Merlin is a guiding force manifesting throughout time with the mission to bring humanity in balance with the land, merging the old ways with the new. So in that sense, Merlin Consciousness was not unlike what we now call Christ Consciousness or Buddhic Consciousness. It represented a particular level of magical awareness some humans could achieve.

The story of Merlin grew out of the oldest accounts we know. He was transformed over time from warrior to wild man and poet, from prophet, to a magician of nature, similar to a shaman. The wild magician was "civilized" into our idea of the courtly wizard. The specific imagery we associate with Merlin today, the dark cloak of stars and planets and the conical hat most likely originates with the figure of Zarathustra, a middle eastern prophet, magician, and teacher. His Persian home is also home to the Magi, the root of our word magician.

Our vision of Merlin as a force of guidance and inspiration is the driving theme of popular tales of Merlin. This version is an amalgam of the most important elements in the story of Merlin.

*Long ago, in a land to the west of London, a wicked king named Vortigern built a tower. The tower was to protect him from the many enemies he made in the land, inviting in Saxon invaders who eventually betrayed him. Everyday his workers would begin construction, and every evening, the tower would collapse. Each day they had to start over again. King Vortigern called for his wizards, who told him the only way to make the tower stay up was to mix the blood of a boy who had no father in with the mortar. Then the tower would be invincible.*

*Vortigern sent his men out to look for such a boy, and they found young Merlin. Merlin was born of a mother and no earthly father. Some say his father was one of the great and noble spirits beyond the Moon, blessing Merlin's mother with a powerful and wise child. Others say his father was a demon, a devil and incubus who preyed upon the fears of his mother and cursed the child with the ability to see beyond time and space. The wise say Merlin's father was a student of the mysteries that lived in the land long before Christianity came to Britain.*

*The king's men brought young Merlin to the tower. And as they prepared to sacrifice him and mix his blood with the mortar to bind the stones, Merlin stopped them. The child told Vortigern that he could see the real reason why the tower fell. Merlin entered a trance and began to prophesize.*

*Merlin saw beneath the tower a large chamber. In the chamber was a lake. Within the lake were two rocks shaking back and forth, causing the tower to fall. Within each of the rocks was a dragon, one red and one white. The dragons hatched from the stones and began to fight. First the white dragon hurt the red, but eventually the red defeated and drove off the white. Merlin said the red dragon was Britain, the white was the Saxons, and predicted that Vortigern* would be slain, replaced by a series of kings, including Ambrosius Aurelianus, Uther Pendragon, and then Arthur Pendragon, who would restore Britain's sovereignty.

King Vortigern's men dug beneath the tower. And indeed they found the cavern. The cavern did have a lake. They drained the lake and found two stones that burst forth and revealed two dragons, red and white. The dragons fought as Merlin predicted, and he was set free. The King was slain as Merlin predicted, with the chain of kings he foresaw replacing Vortigern.

Merlin kept contact with the good folk of the forest, with the spirits of the animals, trees, and stones. Many believe he went mad with grief over a mistake he made that resulted in the death of a loved one. Running wild in the forest, Merlin became the wild man of the forrest, and in his madness found deeper wisdom in nature. He learned the language of the animals and plants. He learned how to read the signs in the stars. He learned how to better bend and shape the forces of nature all around him. He better understood his work in the world.

Merlin visited apple land, or Avalon, and befriended Viviane, the Lady of the Lake, the priestess of the Otherworld, the spiritual inner world, just as he was priest and prophet of the mortal outer world of England. They were partners in the Mysteries, each serving a different role. Some say she was his lover. Others say she was his sister.

After a great battle with the Saxons where many Britons were slain in an ambush, Ambrosius consulted now with an older Merlin about a fitting monument. Merlin led an expedition of men to Ireland, and used his magic to retrieve a circle of stones, setting it up again in England, as Stonehenge. Legend says the stones were first brought to Ireland by giants from Africa.

Ambrosius was slain and his brother Uther became King. Uther fell in love with, or at least lust with, Ygraine, the wife of Gorlois, the Duke of Cornwall. Merlin used his magic to help Uther take the form of Gorlois, and he made love to Ygraine, conceiving their son Arthur. Gorlois was killed by Uther's troops. Merlin came for Arthur, making sure he was raised by a noble knight, and put him in the care of Sir Ector. Uther then married Ygraine.

Arthur grew to young manhood, and when Uther passed and the land was without a king, Merlin used his magic to arrange the test of the Sword in the

Stone. A sword appeared embedded in a stone with instructions that whomever can free the sword would become the King of all England. After many knights and nobles failed, Arthur succeeded, and began his career as king.

When Arthur's first sword was broken, Merlin asked the Lady of the Lake to replace the sword, to forge a bond between the two worlds and reconnect the mysteries of the Sacred King back with the Goddess of the land and water. Merlin took Arthur to the shores of the Lake, and the Lady gave him Excalibur.

Merlin continued to advise Arthur, and was instrumental in the development of his kingdom, Camelot, and the building of the Round Table and its order of knights. While Arthur was in good relationship with the Goddess, and her earthly representative in his court, his Queen Gwenievere, all was good in the kingdom. Prosperity and protection flourished in the land, for the King and the land are one. When things were unwell between the King and the Queen, disharmony and blight ruled, creating the Wasteland, where nothing would grow or bloom, and strife and misfortune were common. England wasted away physically and spiritually, cut off from the love and blessing of the Goddess. The Knights of the Round Table were sent forth on the quest for the Holy Grail.

The Holy Grail was seen as the cup of Jesus, from the Last Supper. Christian knights believed it would redeem the land in the name of Christ. The grail might have been the Christian cup, but the grail was many things. It was the cauldron of inspiration and immortality of the Goddess. It was a stone that fell from heaven. It was the severed head of an ancient sacred king. It was a spear that bled. The grail would appear to each in its own way. Unknown to the questing knights, they simply had to ask, "Whom does the grail serve?" upon finding it and the land would be restored. The principle of service to each other, the land, the gods, and spirits would be restored. The rose would bloom in the Wasteland.

Sadly, Arthur and the knights were bereft of Merlin's sage counsel. Arthur was defeated by his bastard son Mordred and mortally wounded. Arthur was taken by three Queens to the Isle of Avalon to sleep and heal until he is ready to rise again. England, and the world, fell into a chaos from which it has never quite recovered.

*Merlin's apprentice, some say Nimue, a Lady of the Lake in training, others
say Arthur's half-sister Morgana, seduced him. She tricked Merlin into
revealing all his secrets and then used those secrets to imprison him. His prison
is a tower of glass, a Hawthorne tree, a stone tomb, or a crystal cave. Like the
Holy Grail, Merlin's enclosure looks like different things to different people.
There with him are the Thirteen Treasures of Britain, the sacred artifacts he
saves for the true spiritual king of Britain, Arthur, who will return.*

*Perhaps Merlin is still there. Perhaps he is free. Perhaps he was not tricked
at all, but knew his time for direct influence in the world of humanity was over,
and retired to offer aid in more subtle ways. Perhaps he has initiated other
Merlins in the outer world, to guide us closer to where the King and the land are
one again.*

What are the themes of Merlin's life? Many of these themes are quite
familiar to our other two wise men, demonstrating a parallel process all
three have experienced to gain their particular insights.

Merlin was of unusual birth, having an earthly mother but no
human father. Sounds quite similar to Jesus. In older stories, the Merlin,
who is more warrior turned prophet than magician, was born to royalty,
perhaps even a king himself before he abdicated his throne in grief and
madness.

He spent quite a bit of time in nature as a nomad, wandering in the
forest due to some deep guilt. Some stories say he was driven mad by
being involved in acts of war. Others say his actions got his nephew
killed. While the Merlin stories that start with him as a child credit his
powers to his birth and father, the older tales credit his time in the forest
as the source of his prophetic and magical powers. Many consider the
figure of Merlin to be at least two, if not more, separate characters, with
the child Merlin of the Arthurian cycle and a "mad" Merlin of the forests
of the northern woods. Merlin appears to be an identity that transcends
such individuality, sometimes referred to as *The* Merlin, like The Buddha
or The Christ. When one connects to the Merlin consciousness and
through Pagan initiation reaches a new stage of consciousness, the only
answer to those on this path is "who?" is The Merlin.

In either case, Merlin appears to be a shamanic figure in the Celtic tradition. Shamans are the medicine people of their tribe, who specifically learn to heal by communing with the spirits and with nature. Shamans are in tune with nature, and are "chosen by the spirits." They experience an illness or madness that results in a time of isolation, often in the wild, where they discover their abilities and are trained by the spirits directly in the magical arts. Myrddin's name relates to the water, sometimes translated as "water-man" or "maritime fortress" for the cities on the western shore. Water is traditionally seen as a gateway to the spirits, and in Celtic culture, the land of the dead was always towards the Western sea. Merlin's name is also associated with birds, specifically Falcons. Falcons are shamanic birds, associated with messages between the spirit world and the realm of mortals. The European traditions are ripe with images of "feathered cloaks" for magicians and gods, symbolizing their flight to other worlds.

In Celtic culture, the Druids were the priestly caste that held the mysteries of magic, religion, philosophy and history for the people. With the rise of Christianity in the Celtic territories, Druidism was discouraged and eventually wiped out. What little survived became fused with the Celtic Christian church and the poets and bards. Arthur's Merlin lived at the time of this transition, straddling the line between the Pagan and Christian eras. Many believe, as I do, that the mysteries of Merlin and the mystery of the Druids are connected.

When answering the question of "when", the Merlin consciousness manifests most strongly in times of great transition and the strife that occurs when opposing worldviews clash as they become more polarized. No wonder Merlin is so popular with books, movies, and television shows these days, as we appear to be in another societal clash of polarities.

In fact, in one mythic story of Jesus, it is said that as a child he traveled to the British Isles and studied with the Druids, and that is why Joseph of Arimathea brought the cup of the Last Supper to England as a holy relic to be worked with the mysteries of Britain. This connects, at least esoterically, the mythologies of the Druids with the Christians.

Though few neo-Druids today take inspiration from this story, many modern Celtic Christians see it as reason to incorporate reverence for nature and the Goddess back into their religion.

If the Druids fulfilled a role similar to the shaman, albeit in a more organized tradition and body, it's important to understand the role of shamans to understand Merlin. Shamans are not just armchair philosophers or simple priests. They are practitioners of magic. They perform magic and are judged on the results and effects of their magic. They act as intermediaries between the world of humanity and the world of the spirits, both the unseen spirits and the spirits in nature. Embracing the identity of the magician—the prophet-poet, shaman, and priest—to answer the question of "what", Merlin becomes the intermediary and guide for others. He opens the way for those immersed in the physical world, to listen to the wisdom of nature and the spirits.

Merlin was betrayed, another familiar theme. Usually the stories portray a female apprentice who tricks him in some way, into confinement. If Merlin was as powerful as believed, a prophet who can see the future and the source of power for the apprentice, how did he get tricked? Perhaps there is a larger meaning to the story forgotten by most who are strictly thinking on the human level.

Just as many people cannot understanded the idea of self-sacrifice for others, such as in the story of Jesus, the same cannot understand voluntarily shutting yourself away from the world, to gain a different perspective. Merlin's prison is also known as his enclosure, a glass castle where he can see the stars and prophesize, or "molting cage" called Esplumor, identifying him with a falcon, and the idea that he must molt, shed his feathers, and become something new. His imprisonment implies an evolution or metamorphosis, much like a cocoon is a "prison" for a caterpillar, but ultimately gives birth to a butterfly, the next stage in the life cycle. What has the cocoon of Merlin given birth to? What has he or will he become?

The most important theme in the story of Merlin is that of service. In the traditional Arthurian vision, all Merlin does is in service to the land, the Goddess, and the King, for the King and the land are one. If you help one, you help the other, and bringing the King, and thereby the people, into right relationship with the land where they live is the highest form of service Merlin can perform. That is the reason "why" he does what he does, even when his actions are mysterious.

Merlin is a magician. Magicians listen to the world around them and manifest their will, their vision, in the world. That is the essence of magic, speaking and listening to the world. This is the source of the bard and prophets inspiration. He does so in service to the world. Prophets give voice to the spirits of nature and the Otherworld. Merlin becomes an oracle for them, not only predicting the future, but declaring what shall be in order for the land to be restored.

The first prophecy, with the red and white dragons, was in service of restoring the rightful King. Vortigern was corrupt, and his rule brought misery. Merlin declared the succession that led Britain back to a brighter future. In these stories, Britain can be seen as an allegory for the human world. Restore Britain and you restore the world. In esoteric tradition, Britain is seen as a microcosm, a smaller picture of the larger world. In the tales of Atlantis, the power systems of the world, the ley lines, were said to shift after the cataclysm, and Britain's lines became a hub for influencing the world, leading up to the rise of the British Empire and the dominance of English as a world language. When answering the question "where", Merlin finds the microcosm, where the most change can be effected through smaller local movements. He does not need to travel the world to affect it.

The red and white dragons are two nations on one level, but on the higher level, they are the opposing forces that are part of the inner conflict of humanity, and its struggle to now achieve balance with the land. Many sacred sites associated with dragons were considered great temples to the Goddess. The slaying of the dragon was really a myth to describe the fall of Paganism to institutions of Christianity.

Merlin arranges for the birth of Arthur, envisioning the strongest blood lines to contribute to the new King. Merlin does not pursue his own power and rule for himself, but serves the new young king as advisor and mentor, and designer of Camelot. As a supernatural agent, he never forces his will upon humanity. Despite his wisdom, he knows that humanity must choose to live in harmony with the land. Forced actions will be worthless. Even his withdrawal can be seen as form of service, removing his influence, and the idea that no matter what we do to screw up, Merlin, or someone else, will "save" us. In the end, the lesson of any magician is that we must do for ourselves. We can work with others, and share a vision, but no one can do our part for us. We each have a role to play. We must take action. Even when we stumble and make mistakes, we learn. Only through our work in the world can we find our Divine Will and live in harmony with it.

# Chapter Seven:
# The Practices of Buddhism

While it has become trendy to cite Buddhism as a spiritual influence amongst people who are looking beyond conventional religion, the fact that it is not just a philosophy, but a living practice to put into daily life, escapes many people. Buzz words like "compassion" and "non-attachment" become the pop culture face of Buddhism, and while they are two core tenets, Buddhism in all its many forms is actually quite rich in philosophy, practice, and mysticism. The application of the tenets of Buddhism to your life is really what makes one a Buddhist. Unlike the tenets of more familiar religions to Westerners, simple belief is not a requirement, as it's not a religion of belief. While many of us believe the eastern religions are more passive in practice, it takes quite a bit of work to reach such a place of surrender.

While all branches of Buddhism are descended from Siddhartha, like any other religion, there have been schisms and groups with different interpretations. Most scholars recognizes two major branches of Buddhism: the Theravada, or School of the Elders, and the Mahayana, or "Great Vehicle" of Buddhism, referring to the journey to liberation. Tibetan Buddhism, probably a branch more familiar to Westerner, is part of the Mahayana school.

Within these two major branches of Buddhism are many subsets. The different schools of Buddhism vary on the veracity of specific texts, the path and nature of liberation, and the practices that best achieve it. Buddhist practice can include mindfulness, meditation, physical exercises, devotion, reading scriptures, making invocations, conducting ceremonies, and living a monastic life.

The simple overview of Buddhist practices in this chapter is on basic tenets agreed upon by the majority of Buddhists. We will not delve far into the more esoteric or controversial points dividing the various schools of Buddhist philosophy and practice.

## The Three Jewels

Regardless of branches, one thing separating Buddhists from non-Buddhists is "taking refuge" or guidance and aid from the Three Jewels of Buddhism: Buddha, Dharma, and Sangha. The Three Jewels are known as the Three Treasures or Three Refuges, and even the Triple Gem. Declaration to seek refuge in them is really what makes a Buddhist a Buddhist, instead of a Christian, Hindu, or Muslim. The Three Jewels are:

- **Buddha:** Buddha can obviously reference the founder of Buddhism, Siddhartha, but this jewel also refers to our own Buddha nature, the higher potential of every human being to reach the same state of liberation that Siddhartha did.
- **Dharma:** Dharma means "right action." While dharma can have a different meaning in the context of Hinduism, in Buddhism Dharma refers to the teachings of the Buddha, the texts that help us achieve right action.
- **Sangha:** Sangha is the community. Just like the other terms, it has multiple meanings. On the overt level it refers to the community of practicing Buddhists who help support you on the journey. On a deeper mystical level, it is the community of entities who have attained Buddha-hood, or liberation already, and have led the way for current Buddhists to also succeed.

## The World of the Buddhists

From the teachings of Siddhartha, Buddhists take "refuge" in the Three Jewels because of their particular view on the nature of the world and spirit. Buddhists look at the world as we know it as a place of impermanence. Everything changes. Nothing stays the same. Everything is in flux. The very nature of the world is change, and trying to stop that is like trying to stop the world. Humans, by our very nature, get attached to the things we like and desire, and resist change. This resistance to change is the cause of suffering in our individual lives, and in the world collectively.

These changes in the human realm are the result of karma, the Law of Cause and Effect. In other traditions, Cause and Effect might relate to the forces of a larger cosmos of actions and reactions, but in Buddhism, karma most often refers to the actions of body, word, and mind that results from mental intentions. These intentions plant seeds that bear karmic "fruits" in the future.

The term karma creates a lot of confusion, as different religious traditions use the same word differently. While many modern westerners use the term karma, they most often use it to imply a divine system of reward and punishment. Good people get good things, while bad people, who do bad things, get punished, or negative karma. From an Eastern perspective, or even simply a magical perspective, it is not about punishment and reward, but about the results of your intentions and actions. While karma can be defined as negative and positive, either kind of karma can prevent you from liberation and spiritual enlightenment, as any karma can keep you bound in the world and attached. There is really no such thing as "good" karma. What we label "good" is simply the more pleasing results to our actions. While some schools of Buddhism see this karma as impersonal and unalterable, something that must be played out due to past actions, others have specific practices to reduce "negative" karma and thereby suffering. Meditation, recitation of mantras, the study of sacred texts, and even the invocation of particular Buddhas and Bodhisattvas can reduce and even clear unwanted karma.

Sentient beings desire to gain pleasure and joy and avoid pain and suffering. In Buddhist terms, we are controlled by these desires and not free, or liberated. While controlled, these forces give rise to the Cycle of Samsara, the cycle of suffering and rebirth. It is a perpetuated cycle that continues an existence conditioned by desire and attachment, rather than liberation. The aim of Buddhism is liberation by limiting and then eradicating the forces that perpetuate the Cycle of Samsara.

Buddhists believe the cycle gives rise to rebirth, though their concept of rebirth might be different from that of a Hindu, or an occultist. Most non-Buddhists believe in some form of soul, an individual nature, and most non-Buddhists who believe in reincarnation believe this individual entity transmigrates from one existence to the next, reincarnating into another physical vessel. While Buddhists do subscribe to the doctrine of rebirth, they do not believe in an individual or eternal soul. Instead, they believe in non-self.

The concept of "self" arises from the mind, and cannot be true. Nothing is simply "yours". That is a perception arising from the attachments of the mind. Rebirth in the Cycle of Samsara is a function of "dependent arising". Each new incarnation is the result of a previous incarnation, inheriting its karmic seeds, but there is no transmission of an individual self.

I know, even as a student of worldwide wisdom, I had a hard time making the distinction and truly understanding this teaching until a Buddhist taught me the analogy of the candle flame. As a candle runs low, one can take a taper to it and carry its flame to a new candle. The newly lit candle is not the same candle as the old candle that has now been extinguished, but the new candle has inherited the flame of the old. The new candle is the result of the old, and would not be lit without the previous source of flame, but it is not the same individual candle. While the flame is from the same source, it is not the same exact flame on a different candle "body."

Buddhist believe rebirth can take place within one of six realms, each with their own level of being. The realms are known as:

- **Naraka Beings:** Naraka means "Hell" and these are the beings who dwell in many "hells." Hell doesn't mean quite the same as it does in a Christian context, but the hells are seen as places of suffering, lower worlds you would want to escape and incarnate onto a higher plane.
- **Animals:** One can incarnate as an animal, sharing the world with humanity, but not the same qualities and capacities as humanity.
- **Preta:** Preta is a realm of invisible spirits that also share space with humanity and the animals, but most often go unnoticed. The hungry ghosts of Buddhism are found within the level of the Preta. They are considered to undergo more suffering than the average human,

having strong desires, craving and pains, and may be the ghosts of humans who had those attributes in life.

- **Humans:** The realm of humans is the one we are most familiar with, and is a realm from which attaining liberation through Nirvana is possible.
- **Asuras:** Asuras are the lower deities of Buddhism, sometimes described as Titans and other times demons. While not necessarily "evil" they are like elder gods, not always predisposed to aid humanity, or at least all of humanity, much like the Titans are the elder, more primal gods of Greece, when compared to the newer and more civilized Olympians.
- **Devas:** Devas include the gods and goddesses, which are not seen as supreme in Buddhism, but simply another order of living entities on their own path of enlightenment. Devas are sometimes translated as "angels."

Each of these realms can be further subdivided in the esoteric Buddhist teachings.

Together, the teachings on impermanence, suffering, and the nature of the non-self are known as the Three Marks of Existence. Buddhist practices are aimed at becoming aware of these three fundamental aspects of reality. As most people are unaware of these three marks, the teachings help illustrate them in day-to-day living.

## Liberation

Liberation is the goal of the Buddhist, freedom from cravings and the cycle of suffering through awareness. Each seeks to "awaken" to their own Buddha-hood, like Siddhartha under the Bodhi Tree. Liberation is described as Nirvana. Nirvana technically means extinction or cessation, referring to the end of ignorance, craving (passion and hatred), and delusion. Various sects of Buddhism subdivide the meaning of Nirvana in terms of enlightenment and awakening, making the term more all-encompassing or less, depending on the sect.

Those who have achieved this liberation are referred to as Bodhisattvas, and the Mahayana branch puts great emphasis on the them. Generally they are individuals who achieve liberation from ignorance, craving and delusion, but compassionately wait from entering Nirvana because they seek to use their wisdom to aid the liberation of all sentient beings. Some view Bodhisattvas as embodied, incarnate individuals, while others see them as transcended or ascended beings beyond the world of shape and form. Mahayana Buddhists, including Tibetan Buddhism and Zen Buddhism, encourage practitioners to take the Bodhisattva vow to aid the liberation of all, not just the self, and are said to practice six "perfections" known as giving, morality, patience, joyous effort, concentration, and wisdom.

While forms of Buddhism encourage reverence and spiritual contact with these Bodhisattvas, they should not be substituted for the eternal aim of liberation in Buddhism. Zen Buddhism has a particularly wise and poignant saying, "If you meet the Buddha on the road, kill him."

This saying is not a strange call for violence, but rather is a metaphorical teaching. On the road, the path of life, we encounter many people, ideas, and experiences. It is easy to venerate them as the "way" on the road. We often elevate physical teachers as well as those from our mythos. We might have an idea of what it means to be a Buddha. Whenever we encounter such concepts, even when embodied in people, we must destroy them, as they are distractions on the path. It doesn't mean we destroy or kill the people, but we kill our ideal images, and our total reverence of them. We can get attached to the ideas, images, and expectations of another. Teachers should be guides and mentors, not goals unto themselves. Technically the Buddha himself is not considered a deity, and if he has reached liberation, is beyond the call of prayer as an entity. All he has done is shown the way for us to go, but cannot help us even if we call upon him. While he has attained full Buddha-hood, some more mystical sects of Buddhism still petition him like a Bodhisattva, though such petitions were never a part of his original teachings.

If we can totally conceptualize Buddha-hood or enlightenment before we reach it, then we have missed the mark and do not truly understand it. When we do reach it, there will be no need to conceptualize or communicate it. It simply will be.

# The Teachings of the Buddha

To attain the awakening and liberation of the Buddha, Siddhartha left specific teachings to guide us on the path. They are boiled down to two basic sections, to be followed as the Middle Way, a path of non-extremes. The first is known as the Four Noble Truths. The Four Noble Truths sum up the nature of reality and the remedy for suffering. They are not believed to be personal truths, but the true nature of the world and how it operates, rather than how we believe it operates.

## The Four Noble Truths
1. Life means Suffering
2. The Origin of Suffering is Attachment
3. The Cessation of Suffering is Possible
4. The Path leads to the Cessation of Suffering

The first Noble Truth sums up that to be alive in the world is to suffer. Nothing is perfect, neither humanity nor the world itself. All things are impermanent, so impermanence by its very nature is imperfect. From this point of view, if it was perfect, it would not change. To live in the cycle of change is to suffer, as our nature is generally to avoid change, as change of circumstance can lead to ending conditions of pleasure and starting conditions of pain. We crave pleasures and seek to avoid pain. If we are in the cycle of life, we will invariably experience illness, old age, and loss, and all things that promote suffering. Nothing we achieve, even our happiness, is permanent and thereby open to the creation of more suffering.

The second Noble Truth tells us that the reason why we suffer during change is because we seek to hold onto things permanently, and the world's very nature is impermanence. We get attached to what we want to have and create, and attached to avoiding the things that bring displeasure, pain, and suffering. That is not always possible and in fact, for most of us, it is rarely possible, so we suffer. If we didn't feel attached to fulfilling our craving and avoiding our fears, we would not suffer. We would experience both extremes freely and not get stuck in any point, causing suffering. Loss is inevitable, and as long as we desire to avoid loss, and hope it is possible to avoid loss, we'll suffer.

The third Noble truth gives us hope in the world of the Buddhist. This truth tells us that detachment is possible. We can end our clinging to the world, end our cravings of attachment, and attain a level of awareness without suffering. It is possible.

The fourth and final Noble Truth tells us that the way to end attachment, to end suffering, is through the Path or the "Way". Specifically this refers to the teachings of Buddha. The Path is the Middle Path between the extremes of hedonism and self-mortification. The Path sees the illusions between extremes and finds the balanced point where the end of suffering is possible. In many ways, the tale of Siddhartha's life was about his navigating the path between extremes until he attained Nirvana. The Path is detailed in the second major teaching, the Noble Eightfold Path.

## The Noble Eightfold Path

The Noble Eightfold Path is eight points of action that, according to Buddha, end suffering. They are divided into three categories: wisdom, ethical conduct, and mental development. Along with the Four Noble Truths, they are the Dharma, the right action of the Buddha that is the second of the Three Jewels. The eight points are:

Right View
Right Intention
Right Speech
Right Action
Right Livelihood
Right Effort
Right Mindfulness
Right Concentration

*Right View* pertains to our view of reality, to see it correctly as it truly is, not as it appears to be as we we want it to be. Right view includes an understanding and acceptance of the Four Noble Truths as the right view of the world. Right View is not a function of intellect or education, but an intuitive understanding, and is thus considered one of the two wisdom teachings of the eight. Right View leads us to the other seven points of the Path.

*Right Intention* is the second wisdom teaching, referring to the intention, or mental energy, behind our actions. It is a commitment to the other six points on the Path. Buddha included three specific intentions on the Path, the intention of renunciation, to renounce or abandon your desires, the intention of good will, including a freedom from anger, and lastly an intention of harmlessness, not to think or act cruelly but instead develop compassion.

*Right Speech* refers to the power of words, as words can be used to heal or harm, to save or to kill. Those committed to Right Speech only use their words to speak in a truthful and non-hurtful way. Though the balance between truthful and non-hurtful is difficult, as the truth often hurts, the Buddhist is encouraged to not only abstain from lies and deceit, but from harsh and hurtful words and idle chatter that is unnecessary, as well as to speak directly and warmly. Right Speech is the first of the Ethical principles of conduct, for it is the first point that decidedly governs action in the world, not just an intention or perception.

*Right Action* is the second ethical principle and parallels Right Speech. One is encouraged to act in the world in a wholesome and sound manner, refraining from harming others, intentionally or accidentally. One cannot rob, steal, take a life, or have sexual conduct that would harm another.

As the third ethical principle, *Right Livelihood* dictates the manner in which one earns a living and should be in harmony with the previous precepts. It must not harm another, being both legal and peaceful. The Buddha gave four examples of things to be avoided in our vocations in order to conduct Right Livelihood: dealing in weapons, dealing in living beings (including humans and livestock), meat production, and selling alcohol, drugs, or poison.

*Right Effort* refers to the expenditure of mental and physical energy in order to improve upon the Path. It is the first of the mental disciplines required. Our effort must be wholesome and in harmony with the other precepts. Basically, one is called to create and sustain wholesome states and prevent and abandon unwholesome states as they arise.

Clear consciousness, to see things as they are in every moment, without attachment or craving, is the goal of *Right Mindfulness.* You must be aware of yourself and the world around you. We take in data about ourselves and the world around us, and interpret it without clarity to the actual phenomenon, clouded by our past experiences, beliefs, hopes, and fears, in essence our attachments. Right Mindfulness encourages us to operate from a place of clarity when observing ourselves and the world, to better enact the other precepts. It is the second of the mental disciplines.

The last of the mental disciplines is *Right Concentration.* It is the process of focus and meditation. Meditation is the discipline that builds up our powers of concentration, giving us the ability in and out of meditation, to be single-pointed at the task at hand. Buddhists are encouraged to be focused upon wholesome actions, and ultimately the attainment of Buddha-hood through liberation. If you are not focused on the attainment in a wholesome manner, you will wander, with no purpose, suffering needlessly.

There are many other teachings in Buddhism, including the Precepts, that can be considered expansions upon the Four Noble Truths and the Eightfold Path. These provide the foundation for most Buddhist Traditions, considered direct teachings from Siddhartha after his awakening.

## The Practice of Buddhism

While the teachings of Buddha can seem like intellectual ideals, without religious rituals and rites attached to them, this is untrue. The various sects of Buddhism all have their own practices, drawn from the sacred scriptures, with some more esoteric than others. The most well-known of these comes from Tibetan Buddhism. Meditation in any form marks the transition of Siddhartha meditating under the Bodhi tree to reach his state of awakening.

Even if one is not culturally Buddhist, living and learning in Buddhist community, one can benefit from the wisdom practices of Buddhism and incorporate them into your life.

## Mindfulness

One of the eight points on the Path, Right Mindfulness is a primary practice in and of itself, understood by its practical application. There are four foundations of mindfulness, four aspects to contemplate in order to be aware and mindful.

Contemplation of the Body
Contemplation of the Feelings
Contemplation of the State of Mind
Contemplation of the Phenomena

In any given moment, are you aware of these four distinct foundations? They affect our perceptions and our ability to enact the other points of the Eightfold Path.

What are you feeling physically, physiologically, in your body? Are you energized or tried? Are you sore? Are you full or hungry? Is anything strained? Are you feeling any pleasurable or painful sensations? Are there any sensations at all? What is the physical sensory information you are receiving through your sense of sight, hearing, smell, taste and touch? Are you present in your body at all? Many of us, particularly those of us who believe ourselves "spiritual", often disassociate from our body in favor of our thoughts and fantasies. In Buddhism, you must be clear and present in the body while remaining unattached.

What are you feeling emotionally? How would you characterize that emotion? Are you attracted, repulsed, or neutral to whatever experience you are having? Is there any correspondence between your emotion, your feeling, and your physical body? Buddhists learn to observe the emotions, the flow of emotions through day-to-day life, without getting any attachment or sense of identity from the emotions or their exchange.

What is your state of mind? How would you describe it? Are you aware and clear? Are you clouded? Is your physiology affecting your mind by any substances eaten or imbibed? Awareness is key.

What is the state of whatever you are observing? Can you observe and be aware of the true state of the phenomena, or are your other awarenesses clouding your perception of what is before you?

Mindfulness of all four foundations is more difficult than you might imagine. Each leads to its own branches of contemplation and meditation techniques.

## Inviting the Bell

Inviting the Bell is a simple ritual found in some forms of Buddhism. It uses a bell, or more appropriately, what most in the West see as a metal singing bowl, to bring our awareness back to the present moment and be mindful. Often called Tibetan Singing bowls, they are actually manufactured in several countries, including Nepal. The metal of the bowls is traditionally a seven metal alloy of gold, silver, iron, tin, copper, lead, and zinc, similar to the seven planetary metals of the ancients, but substituting zinc for quicksilver.

The bell is gently "awakened" with a very light but firm tap of the wood stick to the rim of the bell, holding it there, preventing the full sound of the bell. This is followed by a second, stronger tap and then finally a third, fully "awakened" bell. The awakening of the bell, and the awakening of consciousness back to the present moment is akin to reminding us of the awakened state of the true Buddha.

Such singing bowls can be "sung" by circling the wooden stick around the rim of the bowl and gently supporting the bottom with your palm or a pillow, to let it ring continuously as if it were singing. The mind can be focused on the bright sound of the bowls. Mystically, each tone of the various sized bowls is said to stimulate one of the energy centers in the body.

## Breath Meditation

Breath meditation is a simple practice found in many Buddhist traditions and in many other meditation techniques, religious and secular. A technique to be mindful of the body and the mind is through breath. A change in your mindset alters your breathing pattern. A change in breathing patterns can change the state of mind of the breather. Breath meditation is known as Anapanasati in Buddhism, meaning "Mindfulness of Breath." When practiced as a part of the Noble Eightfold Path it is said to purify the practitioner of any "kilesa" or defilements and can lead to nirvana. Anapanasati is a particularly important technique in the Theravada schools of Buddhism.

The first type of breathing meditation in Buddhism is to simply observe your breath. Sit in a comfortable position and notice the length of the inhale and the length of the exhale. There is no judgement on what is a good or bad breath. The goal is not a long or short breath. Just observe.

Another simple technique for breathing meditation is to count the breaths. As before, sit in a comfortable position and either count your breaths at the start of every inhale or at the end of every exhale.

Going beyond simple breath work, Buddhist meditation with breath can be expanded into specific steps. Anapanasati is divided into four sections, known as Satipatthanas, which are each divided into four sections, creating sixteen phases. A practitioner performing Anapanasati should go through all states in order, even if not previously successful with all the stages in other meditation sessions.

### Contemplation of the Body
1. Breathing long
2. Breathing short
3. Experiencing the whole body
4. Tranquilizing the bodily activities

### Contemplation of Feelings
5. Experiencing rapture
6. Experiencing bliss

7. Experiencing mental activities

8. Tranquilizing mental activities

## Contemplation of the Mind

9. Experiencing the mind

10. Gladdening the mind

11. Centering the mind in Samadhi

12. Releasing the mind

## Contemplation of Dharmas

13. Contemplating impermanence

14. Contemplating fading of lust

15. Contemplating cessation

16. Contemplating relinquishment

This type of meditation, starting with the breath, puts the four foundations of mindfulness into a more formalized practice.

## Chanting

Chanting is a large part of Buddhist practice. Chanting focuses the mind on specific syllables, words considered to have power, and the ability to prevent harm and promote awareness. Many chants are from the words of the Buddha himself. The practice of chanting in Buddhism most likely comes from the mantra traditions of India.

The most famous of the Buddhist chants comes from the Tibetan Buddhist tradition and is particularly important to the devotees of the Dali Lama.

*Figure 2: Om Mani Padme Hum (Tibetan Characters)*

*Buddha, Christ, Merlin*

This is translated as the "Jewel in the Lotus" and is the six syllable mantra for Avalokiteshvara, the Bodhisattva of Compassion. The Dali Lama is said to be an incarnation of Avalokiteshvara. The text in Tibetan script appears on prayer flags in Tibet or carved upon rocks and has become popular outside of the traditions of Tibetan Buddhism. Influenced by Hindu traditions, the words are usually translated as

*Om:* Creation, Sustainment, and Destruction
*Mani:* Jewel
*Padme:* Lotus
*Hum* (**or** *Hung*)**:** Indivisibility or Inseparability

Om is the power of creation in its three aspects, and also refers to the body, speech, and mind that is perfected in a Buddha. The jewel in the physical world relieves us of poverty, while the jewel in this chant relieves us of spiritual poverty, removing the difficulties of cyclical existence. The lotus is the symbol of wisdom, the wisdom of realized emptiness beyond the world of duality. Hum is the inseparability of the one, the undifferentiated entity that is all. This mantra's six syllables are also said to correspond to the six Samsaric realms of rebirth.

Recite this chant out loud or silently. It can bring peace and joy, relieve karma, gather merit, and relieve suffering.

The chanting of a few of the Bodhisattvas' names ritually can help attune a practitioner to the qualities of that Bodhisattva.

- *Namo Shakyamunaye Buddhaya* (Chant the name of The Fully Awakened Buddha three times and then strike bell.)
- *Namo Amitabhaya Buddhaya* (Chant the name of The Buddha of Infinite Light three times and then strike bell.)
- *Namo Manjushriye Bodhisattvaya* (Chant the name of The Bodhisattva of Great Understanding three times and then strike bell.)
- *Namo Samantabhadraya Bodhisattvaya* (Chant the name of The Bodhisattva of Great Action three times and then strike bell.)

- *Namo Avalokiteshvaraya Bodhisattvaya* (Chant the name of The Bodhisattva of Great Compassion three times and then strike bell.)
- *Namo Kshitigarbhaya Bodhisattvaya* (Chant the name of The Bodhisattva of Great Aspiration three times and then strike bell.)

Mantra chanting in Hinduism and Buddhism is done with the aid of a *mala*, a beaded necklace of 108 (or 109) beads. One bead is for each repetition of the mantra, 108 is ideall.

## Devotion

Many Buddhists appear to "pray" to statues of the Buddha, making offerings of flowers, coins, or water. Yet Buddhism is not a theistic religion, seeking the intercession of a higher authority. What might look like prayer is usually, depending on the practitioner, culture and circumstance, an act of devotion and veneration. Buddha actually prohibited his followers from worshiping him or making statues, but they eventually became a part of the tradition. Ritualistic traditions that adopted Buddhism adapted their rituals, but retained their outer form. When making an offering of devotion with a wholesome attitude rather than an ulterior motivation for personal benefit, one reflects upon the qualities of the Buddha, the Four Noble Truths, the Eightfold Path, and the precepts of Buddhism. While the ritual has no inherent power to summon otherworldly aid in the Buddhist view, it does help promote concentration and clarity of mind, aiding one on the Path. The five precepts recited are:

Abstain from harming living beings
Abstain from stealing
Abstain from sexual misconduct
Abstain from falsehood
Abstain from intoxicants

## Altars of Veneration

Many people, both in the east and west, have household altars and shrines with an image of Buddha upon them. Rather than worship Buddha, they can be used as reminders of the principles and qualities of a Buddha, and what you aspire to embody. Ritual offerings of flowers, incense, or water can be placed upon the altar in acts of veneration while focusing upon the teaching of Buddha, to kindle strength and awareness to follow the Path.

## Incense Offering

1) Strike bell three times.

2) Light Incense, for example, Joss sticks.

3) Recite:

> *In gratitude, we offer this incense*
> *throughout all space and time*
> *to all Buddhas and Bodhisattvas.*
> *May it be fragrant as Earth herself,*
> *reflecting careful efforts,*
> *wholehearted awareness,*
> *and the fruit of understanding,*
> *slowly ripening.*
> *May we and all beings*
> *be companions of Buddhas and Bodhisattvas.*
> *May we awaken from forgetfulness*
> *and realize our true home*

4) Strike bell once.

## Zen Koan

The koan is a literary teaching device found in Zen Buddhism, though its history predates Buddhism. Unlike many other forms of Buddhism, Zen Buddhism, found largely in China, Korea, Japan, and now America, does not emphasize scriptural study or ritual. Instead it focuses upon meditative exercises, and the use of koans are a part of its practice.

Koans take the form of a question that has no "real" answer, but the question, often representative of a paradox, forces the student to turn off their logical, linear rational mind and access a different source of wisdom to contemplate the answer. Sometimes koans are considered a test for the student, to measure their progress, while other times, simply a teaching device.

Some examples of the more famous and well loved koans include:

### One Hand

*When both hands are clapped a sound is produced; listen to the sound of one hand clapping.*

### What is Buddha

*What is Buddha?*

*Three pounds of flax.*

### A Cup of Tea

*Nan-in, a Japanese master during the Meiji era (1868-1912), received a university professor who came to inquire about Zen. Nan-in served tea. He poured his visitor's cup full, and then kept on pouring. The professor watched the overflow until he no longer could restrain himself. "It is overfull. No more will go in!" "Like this cup," Nan-in said, "you are full of your own opinions and speculations. How can I show you Zen unless you first empty your cup?"*

### No-thing

*A monk asked Joshu, a Chinese Zen master: "Has a dog Buddha-nature or not?"*

*Joshu answered: "Mu." (Mu means "No-thing or Nay in Chinese. It is the negative.)*

### Nothing

*When you can do nothing, what can you do?*

## Bodhisattva Vow

The Bodhisattva Vow is a promise made, often transcending lifetimes, by a sincere and compassionate individual who has generated what is known as *bodhicitta*, the intention to reach Buddha-hood for the enlightenment and betterment of not only the self, but for all beings. In fact, the liberation of all, rather than just the self, is the motivating factor. The vow is found in Mahayana Buddhism, where there are teachings on the Bodhisattva, the beings who have made this vow and ultimately have completed all work necessary to enter into nirvana, but consciously postpone this union to aid others in their own achievement of enlightenment. Some see any who have taken the vow as a Bodhisattva, or simply a Bodhisattva "in training" with the dedication, but not yet the accomplishment.

The term Bodhisattva Vow is usually summed up by a statement such as:

*May I attain Buddha-hood for the benefit of all sentient beings.*

Yet the singular term "vow" is misleading, as many texts lists multiple vows for one seeking to be a Bodhisattva. The Zen tradition of Buddhism has a four-fold vow. The Brahma Net Sutra lists ten major vows and forty eight minor vows. Asanga, the co-founder of the Vasubandhu school of Buddhism lists eighteen major Bodhisattva vows and fourty-six minor vows, which is also used in Tibetan Buddhism.

Some simply take the vow on their own. Others believe it must be done ceremonially with a teacher present. In formal lineage traditions of training, the Bodhisattva vow is preceded by what is known as the Refuge Vow, a ceremonial vow to commit to the Three Refuges. It is the commitment to Buddhism in these traditions.

The Dali Lama conducts a ceremony for those taking the vow, and this is a version he has used:

*With a wish to free all beings*
*I shall always go for refuge*
*To the Buddha, Dharma and Sangha,*
*Until I reach full enlightenment.*
*Enthused by wisdom and compassion,*
*today in the Buddhas' presence I generate*
*the Mind for Full Awakening*
*For the benefit of all sentient beings.*
*As long as space remains,*
*As long as sentient beings remain,*
*Until then, may I too remain*
*And dispel the miseries of the world.*

# The Dalai Lama and Tibet

The Dalai Lama is the leader of the Gelugpa school of Tibetan Buddhism. Gelugpa is the Yellow Hat sect of Tibetan Buddhism, and he is considered the high lama, or "high priest" of the school, but has taken on so much more. While the high lama, he is not officially the leader of Gelugpa, but has appointed one in the office of Galen Trippa to lead the school.

In today's global culture, he is acknowledged as the spiritual leader of Tibetan Buddhism, and often erroneously thought of as the leader of all Buddhists. While he is respected by a great number, he is only officially a spiritual representative of Tibetan Buddhist groups. Tibetan Buddhism is a branch of Mahayana, one of the two major branches of Buddhism, side by side with Theravada Buddhism. Due to the very public nature of Tibet's political and cultural conflict with China, the Dalai Lama has become the public face of Buddhism for many Westerners, who consider Tibet the spiritual home of Buddhism, despite Buddha's actual origin in India.

To his followers and devotees in Tibetan Buddhism, the Dalai Lama is considered to be the incarnation of the Bodhisattva of compassion, Avalokiteśvara. Avalokiteśvara depictions, stories ,and origin vary greatly in the various Buddhist schools and teachings, though they all agree upon his great compassion. Some see him simply as a great Bodhisattva, others a true buddha, and still others a vehicle for a deity of compassion. In one story, to alleviate the suffering of all others, he agrees to incarnate as everyone, living their lives so they may attain nirvana. In Tibetan teaching, he is particularly given the task of caring for Tibet, and manifests or incarnates in a line of tulkas. Tulkas are high ranking lamas who have a measure of conscious control over their next incarnation, and greater memory of past lives and purpose. There is a tradition for the signs of rebirth and the search for an incarnating tulka. Often the new incarnation is tested to identify toys and relics from the previous lives. The Dalai Lama is the most famous tulka, and has stated publicly, much to the difficulty of the Chinese government, that the office of the Dalai

Lama might be abolished, or his next incarnation might be outside of Tibet and the Tibetan people, and might be female.

The current Dalai Lama, Tenzin Gyatso, is believed to be the fourteenth Dalai Lama, an incarnation of the previous thirteen manifestations of Avalokiteśvara. The fifth Dalai Lama took over political control of Tibet, and the current Dalai Lama was considered the head of the true Tibetan government in exile, until his retirement in 2011.

Tibet and China have had a contentious relationship, with at various points in their history, Tibet acting independently, as well as seemingly under China's control. At times past, Tibetans and particularly past Dalai Lamas, were accused of persecuting non-Buddhist Christians in Tibet. But in 1950s, the conflict broadened. After the Chinese Civil War, the People's Republic of China incorporated Tibet into China's overall control, negotiating a seventeen point treaty with the then new, 14th Dalai Lama. By 1959, after famine blamed upon the Chinese government's policies, along with an effort to extinguish Tibet's cultural and religious traditions, an uprising occurred. The Dalai Lama repudiated the seventeen point agreement with China and fled Tibet into India to establish an autonomous Tibet government in exile, and works for the rights of Tibetans both in Tibet and abroad, as both spiritual and political leader. Since that time he has become more and more established as the public face of both Tibet and Buddhism in the west, making a case for support of Tibetan independence among western governments, and compassion and good will for all. Many see the support for a free Tibet as a part of their spiritual practice and part of the path of the betterment of all beings.

## Tantric & Mystical Buddhism

While at face value, the most simple and direct teachings of the Buddha are common, no nonsense instructions on how to live life and escape suffering. Yet since its introduction, various sect of Buddhism have evolved, some absorbing more mystical and magical ideas into their structure and values, making them seemingly different from the core teachings of basic buddhism, even if those core teachings become the foundation stones upon which the mystical teachings hang.

Tantra is often considered to be secret, ritualized sex, and while sex can be an aspect of tantra, it is not the sole focus. The word tantra is under dispute, but has referred to the warp of fabric, to texts, and to mystical rituals. Most commonly used in India as part of various Hindu traditions, the word has later been associated with many other traditions and cultures. In Tibet, many forms of Buddhism both fused with, and competed with, native Tibetan tradition.

The tradition known today as Bön is often represented as the native or indigenous sorcerous traditions of Tibet, while other see it as a competing religion contemporary with, or even later to, Buddhism. Still others feel that the Bön traditions are really now part of the overall Buddhist schools within Tibet. Bön is known to use a wide variety of rituals for not only personal enlightenment, but often more importantly to control outer reality and spirits. Rites will call for changes in the weather, blessings of the land, protection of the home and healing of the sick. Bön is often considered the native Pagan magic of Tibet.

Tantric Buddhism is technically an extension of the Mahayana. Often referred to as *Vajrayana*, meaning "Diamond Vehicle," while Mahayana means "The Great Vehicle." Some think it is a distinct branch, but it is rooted in Mahayana teachings. The Vajra is also the divine thunderbolt of enlightenment, and a ritual tool used to symbolize that thunderbolt. In Tibet the object is called the Dorje. Sometimes two are ritually crossed or one is paired with a ritual bell.

*Figure 3: Vajra or Dorje*

Sexuality and the pairs of sexual couples found in Tantric teachings are alluding to the healing of a duality consciousness within the practitioner, where the self and other become one, as the practitioner and enlightenment become one. All paradox is resolved. Direct experience through the ritual is emphasized, though there are many initiatory lineage traditions of tantric teaching. Gurus or lamas to guide one on the path are still encouraged. Rituals tools, mantras, symbols, mandalas, energy work, visualizations, and unusual actions are all a part of the tantric traditions. Tantric Buddhist practices are often considered a "swift" or "fast" path and that is why it is known as the diamond, or perfected, vehicle.

A common practice is to imagine oneself as a Buddhist deity. You must see yourself as the body of the deity you have chosen. Your environment around you must be seen as the pure land, as represented by the mandala of the deity. You must strive to experience the bliss of the deity with no attachment. And in all these things, you must do it for the benefit of others, the bodhicitta motivation, not for self-gratification. To assume the form of a deity is to assume a form that more people can relate to than your current human form. These are known as the four purities of Buddhist Deity practice.

### Assuming the Form of Avalokiteśvara

Before attempting this practice, it can be helpful to obtain an image or mandala depicting Avalokiteśvara and becoming thoroughly familiar with it. Observe every object of the deity and every aspect of the scenery surrounding him. You can substitute some of the imagery suggested with imagery from the depiction of the Avalokiteśvara you are studying.

*Figure 4: Avalokiteśvara*

Traditionalist Buddhists would suggest not attempting this practice without a full commitment to the Buddhist path, renunciation of the world, refuge in the three jewels, generation of bodhicitta, and a true

*Buddha, Christ, Merlin*

understanding of the emptiness of the world. Yet, the practices are very similar to other magical and esoteric traditions without such beliefs or restrictions. There are dangers to any form of deity yoga, Buddhist or not. One can become obsessed with the image, or conflate the ego with the deity, and lose a sense of self in personal practice. That is why it is essential that the aim be the betterment of all sentient beings.

The practice below is not from a specific form of Tantric Buddhism, but a generalized technique to help the layperson understand and experience the mystical side of Buddhism, particularly from a Tibetan view. If practiced in a specific lineage, there would be a greater ritual structure beyond the visualization. This often has a lengthy recitations of lineage, offerings, invocations to the deity, a veneration of the image generated before merging or arising with it, and an initiation of the deity when you have arisen as it. The following is a suitable introduction for those who might then seek out more formal training in Buddhist tantra.

Get into a comfortable but focused meditation position, such as cross legged with spine erect. If the art of Avalokiteśvara has a particular position that you can assume, assume that posture before beginning and retain it. Focus on the bodhicitta, the altruistic intent of the diamond path.

> I humbly bow to Avalokiteśvara
> Bodhisattva who destroys sorrow, fear and sufferings
> Bodhisattva who has reached perfection
> Bodhisattva who looks to all with forgiveness.
> Avalokiteśvara who is compassion for the world.

Begin reciting the mantra of Avalokiteśvara, *Om Mani Padme Hum*. You can do a round of chanting on the 108 mala beads. Keep the beads with you, as you will envision them as a set of crystal mala beads in the ritual.

Upon completion, envision the mantra syllables transporting you to the clear blue sky, radiant in all directions, infinite and empty. You are free within this blue sky. This is the freedom we all crave and receive when we become equinanimous in our own minds. This is the mindscape of the Bodhisattva.

Beneath you is a throne of jewels. The jewels shine brightly into the blue light. Upon the throne of jewels is a perfect white lotus and within the white lotus a white mat, circular and cool, reminding you of the full Moon. Imagine the sound you had generating in preparation, transforming you into the rainbow body of Avalokiteśvara. Become Avalokiteśvara, as an actual emanation of full awakening and compassion. Your physical body has been replaced by the body of Avalokiteśvara, the body of wisdom, bliss, and compassion. Identify with this new body. Think about how real this is. This is truly who you are, not the body and identity of this life. You are not pretending.

Your body is bright white light. You emanate white light into the blue sky and jewels of your throne. You have four, or perhaps a thousand, arms. Your hands are filled with sacred relics. An inner pair of hands holds the wish fulfilling gem at the heart, the gem of compassion. You have a crystal mala bead strand in one hand, and a lotus flower in another. Your head is covered with blue-black locks of hair, and your mouth forms a perfect smile as you gaze upon the world.

While seemingly alone in the blue sky, we look up and feel the presence of Amaitābha, taking the form of a giant ruby, filled with infinite light. Amaitābha is the guru, the teacher of Avalokiteśvara. While seemingly separate, Avalokiteśvara and Amaitābha are actually connected, and while perhaps not one in the same, the paradox of connection means they are not two separate beings. Our own Avalokiteśvara heart contains the same seed syllable that Amaitābha contains, the syllable Hrīh. We are one with Amaitābha.

Around the heart seed syllable of Hrīh are petals of a lotus with the syllables of *Om Mani Padme Hum.* They are in the colors of white, green, yellow, blue, red, and deep blue. We begin to recite the sound and the wheel of syllables, of petals, spins and turns. As it does, we radiate out infinite compassion to ease the pains, hungers, fears, and cravings. Light goes out into all six realms. White goes to the realm of the gods with the syllable Om. Green goes to the realm of the asuras with Ma. Ni corresponds with yellow, and radiates out into the realm of humans. Pa radiates with blue light to the animals. Dme glows with red light to the hungry ghosts. Hum in the deep blue light goes to the hell realm. With each rotation of the mantra we count off another crystal mala bead. We can continue and actually recite the full 108 mala beads of one set, knowing each bead saves one sentient being and Avalokiteśvara is prepared to say enough mantras to save all sentient beings and liberate all.

When we are complete with this experience, we are sure to offer the merit of the practice to the benefit and liberation of all sentient beings with our sincere attention. Return your awareness to your physical space, knowing that for a time you did become Avalokiteśvara.

As you can see, much of Buddhism, while focusing on detachment, is intellectual, with many teachings, theories, and precepts designed to manage and change the perceptions of the mind, and from those perceptions, the actions cause results in the world of form and spirit. It's a heady system, with many complex ancient texts and modern interpretations in the various sects of Buddhism, as each emphasizes different aspects of Buddha's teachings on the path to liberation. As we progress, you'll find similarities to aspects of Christianity and Paganism, and some major differences too, but Buddhism has the most dominant mental outlook, beginning and ending with the perceptions and attachment/detachment of the mind.

# Chapter Eight:
# The Heart of Christianity

Writing about the practice of Christianity is quite hard for me, as it has been many years since I identified as a practicing Christian. I was born into a Catholic family, and my journey led me away from the dogma and conventions found in the Catholic expression of Christianity. It's ironic, as the true meaning of catholic is "universal," but I found its teachings were not universal for me. To think I could expound upon the teachings of Christ brings up memories of all the old psychological programs that I have carried from my childhood. I know I'm not alone, as many of us carry the baggage and wounding of our birth religion when we strike out to seek wisdom from other sources. But as I approach the heart of the matter, through this book, I feel free. It is because of the truly universal, timeless wisdom traditions and training that goes beyond religion that I am proud to speak on the teachings of Christ.

Spiritual seekers note that many people who do not identify as Christians are the most Christ-like in behavior, for the principles Christ proposed in many of his teachings are a universal wisdom found in the heart of all traditions. Even the rituals we most strongly associate with Christianity, such as the sharing of wine and bread, predate the birth of Christ and are found in Pagan fertility and vegetation religions all across the globe. Many of the mystery traditions of our wisdom still carry the mysteries outside the bounds of the mainstream Christian churches. These teachings, at the heart of the mystery of love, are what I practice, even without the label of Christian.

In examining the tenets and rituals of Christianity, I must admit that no single chapter, in fact, no single book, can adequately outline the differences of all the traditions, philosophies, and theologies in the varieties of Christian faith. They took two thousand years to develop. My own understanding of them is biased and influenced from my childhood experience as an American Roman Catholic. In an effort to look at more of the mystical sides of Christianity, there are generalizations that cannot apply to all the denominations. If you are already comfortable practicing a specific Christian faith, this chapter can provide some ideas to go deeper in your understanding. If you are not already in a specific Christian faith and feel drawn to these teachings of the second ray of Love, then explore a particular denomination that speaks to you, or follow my advice and work with the spirit of the Christ outside of the more restrictive mainstream interpretations. They are more akin to the various strains of mystical and Gnostic Christianity from the earliest era of the faith.

## The Code of Christ

For good or for bad, Jesus left behind no official record of his teachings. If he established set protocols for his mystery teachings and inner circle, they have not survived in a form known to us. What we do have is a series of gospels, testaments about his life and teachings, particularly his public actions and sermons, attributed to his apostles and other followers.

While the four "official" gospels recognized by the Church are credited to the apostles Matthew, Mark, Luke, and John, and comprise the bulk of the Christian New Testament, along with other letters and work authored by the apostles and early saints, there are great scholarly debates on the true historic authors and origins of these teachings. It appears these accounts are written some time after the death of Christ, and while they might have comprised the oral teachings of an apostle, they were probably not first penned by the figure to which they are attributed. In fact one gospel might have inspired or been a source for another. Each of the four, while depicting very similar teachings and events, presents a different view of Jesus and his teachings, and most Christians today recognize a conglomeration of the gospels, rather than specific strains of wisdom from each.

Beyond the accepted gospels there is a wide selection of unofficial Gospels dating from roughly the same time periods and religious practices, but rejected by the early Catholic Church for presenting an aspect of Christ antithetical to the Church's view. These writings are called the New Testament Apocrypha. The Apocrypha generally embodies a more gnostic view of Christ, depicting a more personal and less dogmatic expression of early Christianity, and many modern Christian mystics look to the Apocrypha for inspiration and guidance, to present a new view of Christ beyond the narrow limits of the dominant churches.

From this composite depiction of Christ's message, Christians can draw a code of Christianity. In essence, part of Christ's mission was to simplify the expansive laws of Judaism, starting with the Ten Commandments and continuing with the various moral, social, and religious practices detailing what you should or shouldn't do to be a proper Jew. Some were based in aspects of sanitation and hygiene, other to preserve the culture, and were encoded in religious material to make sure they were taken seriously, for Jewish society is a religious society. It's a hard part for many modern people to understand, with our modern division between religious tenet and secular law. Jesus cleared the misunderstandings around the "shall not's, getting to the heart of what a spiritual person should do. He embodied the living spirit of his philosophy, to expand, explain and amend all the rules of the previous religious cycle in Jewish culture. He specifically said, that he did not come to destroy such rules, but to truly fulfill the heart of them, particularly the prophecies of the Messiah:

*"Do not think that I have come to abolish the Law or the Prophets; I have not come to abolish them, but to fulfill them."* — Matthew 5:17

The following are the generally agreed upon tenets of Christianity, taken from this universal stance on Christ's teaching. Specific denominations agree, disagree, and modify based upon individual theology, and the reason why we have so many Christian denominations is the general lack of agreement among Christian religious leaders to agree upon the main tenets of Christ's message and mission. Theological disagreements have lead to schisms with new rules and dogma, doing the exact opposite of what Christ intended.

## Love

Love is the central teaching of Christ's message. If one were to study the life of Jesus and get no other message, it should be love. Jesus emphasized the love of the divine and transcendent, through emphasizing the love that God the Father has for us, and the love we should have for him, as well as the love people should have for each other.

*And one of the scribes came and heard them arguing, and recognizing that He had answered them well, asked Him, "What commandment is the foremost of all?" Jesus answered, "The foremost is, 'Hear, O Israel! The Lord our God is one Lord; and you shall love the Lord your God with all your heart, and with all your soul, and with all your mind, and with all your strength.' "The second is this, 'You shall love your neighbor as yourself.' There is no other commandment greater than these."* — Mark 12:28:31

*"A new command I give you: Love one another. As I have loved you, so you must love one another. By this all men will know that you are my disciples, if you love one another."*— John 13:34:35

Jesus is asking his followers to embody the same consciousness he embodies, what we know today as "Christ Consciousness", the embodiment of unconditional love. He didn't say to love one another if they are good to you, or do as you say, or agree with you. He simply said "Love one another." His statement is unconditional.

Choosing love is the first step to attaining Christ Consciousness and being more like Jesus, being a true Christian. To choose to love, and the actions that best support love in any situation, is the heart of the Christian tenets. We first choose the love of God, of the Creative force, and from that love we can be supported to choose love in all other situations, with all other people. Our love of the divine should embody four aspects of self: Heart, Soul, Mind, and Strength.

Like the corners of a building, grounding our love in all four keeps us centered and balanced. People forget this specific instruction, and rarely is it expounded upon in more exoteric Christian sermons and teachings. Our heart is our emotions, the feeling of love. Our soul is our personal spiritual essence, the part of us that is most like God. When you can find love in one of these two, the second usually comes along more easily. Likewise, mind and strength can be paired. To love God with your mind is to think love, to make the mental decision for love. From that, we gain strength of body and strength of will to perform whatever is necessary to support and maintain that love.

The four are quite similar to old forms of esoteric mysticism dating back to the ancient Greeks, but finding corollaries in Asian and Indian esoteric medicine, and the teachings of the four elements. More prevalent in magical teachings than Christianity today, the four elements of fire, air, water, and earth played a role in Christian alchemy and Cabala during the Medieval period of Europe. While they are symbolized by parts of nature, they really embody four aspects of our self. Fire is our soul, our life force and energy. Air is our mind. Water is our emotions and earth is our body. When Jesus tells us to love with all our heart, soul, mind, and strength, he is really telling us to love on all levels, with our emotions (water), soul (fire), mind (air) and body (earth). If we can choose the consciousness of love in all four of those areas, by keeping Divinity foremost before us as a focus, we will be closer to attaining a more Christ-like consciousness. Then we can truly go out and love others as Jesus did.

We can't make the mistake of waiting for some miraculous enlightenment from God via our heart, soul, mind, and body to then choose to love others. This divine alchemy occurs simultaneously. When we choose to love other people, and in fact, all people, we come into greater love with the Divine. When we come into greater love with the Divine, we are able to love others more fully, including ourselves. To love others is to see the Divine spark within them. To love your neighbor as yourself is also to see the divine spark within you, and start from a place of self-love and self-esteem. This is one of the mystical paradoxes that are difficult to explain, but speak to the heart of the enlightened experience.

## The Golden Rule

Extending out from the tenet of love comes what is known as The Golden Rule. Although often credited to Christianity exclusively, other cultures and traditions have their own variation of the Golden Rule. In Christianity, it is expressed in the Gospel of Matthew.

*So in everything, do to others what you would have them do to you, for this sums up the Law and the Prophets.* — Matthew 7:12

Other traditions express it in other ways, but essentially say the same thing; treat others as you wish to be treated. If we all follow this basic structure, we have the opportunity for an almost utopian society and create the conditions where the first tenet of love can truly flourish. If we all want to be loved, treat everyone with love and you will receive love in turn. Many of the subsequent teachings of Christianity flow from this Golden Rule.

Here are other versions of this very important tenet, sometimes referred to as the "Prayers of Peace" when gathered together, to show the universality of the concept, beyond the bounds of Christianity:

### Baha'i
And if thine eyes be turned towards justice, choose thou for thy neighbor that which thou choosest for thyself.

### Buddhist
Putting oneself in the place of another, one should not kill nor cause another to kill.

### Confucianism
Never impose on others what you would not choose for yourself.

### Egyptian
That which you hate to be done to you, do not do to another.

### Greek
One should never do wrong in return, nor mistreat any man, no matter how one has been mistreated by him.

*Hinduism*

One should never do that to another which one regards as injurious to one's own self. This, in brief, is the rule of dharma. Other behavior is due to selfish desires.

*Islam*

Hurt no one so that no one may hurt you.

*Judaism*

You shall not take vengeance or bear a grudge against your kinsfolk. Love your neighbor as yourself: I am the LORD.

*Native American*

Give us the wisdom to teach our children to love, to respect, and to be kind to each other; So that they may grow with peace in mind.

*Sikhism*

Whom should I despise, since the one Lord made us all.

*Taoism*

The sage has no interest of his own, but takes the interests of the people as his own. He is kind to the kind; he is also kind to the unkind— for Virtue is kind. He is faithful to the faithful; he is also faithful to the unfaithful—for Virtue is faithful.

*Wicca*

Eight words the Wiccan Rede doth fulfill, And it harm none, do what ye Will.

## Non-Violence

Despite a history which includes empires, crusades, persecutions, and Witch hunts, and the theological justifications of Church elders and Christian politicians, the core teachings of Jesus are of non-violence just as much as any Buddhist sect, even though Buddhists tend to have a stronger interpretation than most Christians.

While in some tales Jesus was prone to outbursts and hyperbole to make his points, he ultimately espoused a path of non-violence, preventing revenge, and in some interpretations, even self-defense if it meant to harm another. His death by ghastly crucifixion was not something he hid from, nor did he use violence to prevent it, or allow any of his followers to use violence. When Jesus is arrested, his apostle Simon Peter tries to stop the servants of Caiaphas by using a sword to cut off his ear. Jesus heals the wound and chastises him for it. He states a now well known saying in Matthew's gospel, "All who live by the sword shall die by the sword."

Jesus' most famous saying on the topic is a reinterpretation of the Old Testament saying on revenge.

*You have heard that it was said, 'eye for eye, and tooth for tooth.' But I tell you, do not resist an evil person. If someone strikes you on the right cheek, turn to him the other also.* — Matthew 5:38:39

This interpretation is radical for many and hard to accept, but ultimately stems from his teachings of love and the Golden Rule. Christ goes on to say more about how to deal with our enemies.

*There is a saying, 'Love your friends and hate your enemies.' But I say: Love your enemies! Pray for those who persecute you! In that way you will be acting as true sons of your Father in heaven. For he gives his sunlight to both the evil and the good, and sends rain on the just and on the unjust too. If you love only those who love you, what good is that? Even scoundrels do that much. If you are friendly only to your friends, how are you different from anyone else? Even the heathen do that. But you are to be perfect, even as your Father in heaven is perfect.* — Matthew 5:43:48

Through loving our enemies, we better comprehend the unconditional nature of God's love for us, as manifest through nature, through sunlight, and through rain. It is only through this unconditional nature do we understand true love, and our enemies become great teachers to us on the lessons of divine and unconditional love.

### Forgiveness

Continuing our thread of the Golden Rule, most people seek forgiveness when transgressing against the divine or against another person. Jesus espouses the principle of forgiveness as divine. In fact, his entire life is interpreted by religious theologians as the sacrifice for the forgiveness of all sins in the redemption and salvation of all people. His own words focus on the personal actions we can take to remember to forgive others so we too will be forgiven. If we do not, we actually place a barrier to love in our hearts and minds, and lose sight of the most important commandments.

*For if you forgive men for their transgressions, your heavenly Father will also forgive you. But if you do not forgive men, then your Father will not forgive your transgressions.* — Matthew 6:14:15

Judgment is an inherent part of forgiveness. Jesus spoke not about giving up our discernment, but the type of judgment that comes with moral superiority. It can prevent us from forgiving others of their failings, and blind us to our own faults and mistakes, preventing us from seeking out forgiveness for ourselves.

*Do not judge, or you too will be judged. For in the same way you judge others, you will be judged, and with the measure you use, it will be measured to you. Why do you look at the speck of sawdust in your brother's eye and pay no attention to the plank in your own eye? How can you say to your brother, 'Let me take the speck out of your eye,' when all the time there is a plank in your own eye? You hypocrite, first take the plank out of your own eye, and then you will see clearly to remove the speck from your brother's eye.* — Matthew 7:1:5

## Charity

Charity is another extension of "do unto others." Jesus strongly encouraged people to give all they had to others. Food, clothing, and shelter should be shared between people, and those with it should share with others as much as they can. Several passages depict this concept of service and charity.

*Jesus sat down opposite the place where the offerings were put and watched the crowd putting their money into the temple treasury. Many rich people threw in large amounts. But a poor widow came and put in two very small copper coins, worth only a fraction of a penny. Calling his disciples to him, Jesus said, "I tell you the truth, this poor widow has put more into the treasury than all the others. They all gave out of their wealth; but she, out of her poverty, put in everything: all she had to live on." —* Mark 12:41:44

*For if you give, you will get! Your gift will return to you in full and overflowing measure, pressed down, shaken together to make room for more, and running over. Whatever measure you use to give—large or small—will be used to measure what is given back to you." —* Luke 6:38

Most importantly, Jesus identifies the Divine in each and every person, showing what you do to your fellow neighbors, "brothers," you do to God. That which you fail to do for others you fail to do to God. There is no difference in your actions towards people and towards God, and in fact your treatment of others is a clear measure of your treatment to the Divine.

*"But when the Son of Man comes in His glory, and all the angels with Him, then He will sit on His glorious throne. "And all the nations will be gathered before Him; and He will separate them from one another, as the shepherd separates the sheep from the goats; and He will put the sheep on His right, and the goats on the left. "Then the King will say to those on His right, 'Come, you who are blessed of My Father, inherit the kingdom prepared for you from the foundation of the world. 'For I was hungry, and you gave Me something to eat; I was thirsty, and you gave Me drink; I was a stranger, and you invited Me in; naked, and you clothed Me; I was sick, and you visited Me; I was in prison, and you came to Me.' "Then the righteous will answer Him, saying, 'Lord, when did we see You hungry, and feed You, or thirsty, and give You drink? 'And when did we see You a stranger, and invite You in, or naked, and clothe You? 'And when did we see You sick, or in prison, and come to You?' "And the King will answer and say to them, 'Truly I say to you, to the extent that you did it to one of these brothers of Mine, even the least of them, you did it to Me.' "Then He will also say to those on His left, 'Depart from Me, accursed ones, into the eternal fire which has been prepared for the devil and his angels; for I was hungry, and you gave Me nothing to eat; I was thirsty, and you gave Me nothing to drink; I was a stranger, and you did not invite Me in; naked, and you did not clothe Me; sick,*

*and in prison, and you did not visit Me.' "Then they themselves also will answer, saying, 'Lord, when did we see You hungry, or thirsty, or a stranger, or naked, or sick, or in prison, and did not take care of You?' "Then He will answer them, saying, 'Truly I say to you, to the extent that you did not do it to one of the least of these, you did not do it to Me.' "* — Matthew 25:31:45

If you seek to walk a Christian path, you give selflessly to others in a spirit of charity.

## Poverty

One of the less popular teaching of Jesus, yet found in several gospels, is the concept of poverty. Many religious traditions, east and west, have concepts of poverty and renouncement of material goods, particularly for clergy, as they distract from the devotion of spirit. Ironically, many Christian institutions are among the richest in the world, with the concept that no individual holds all the wealth, but it's kept in common property. The communities of early followers gave rise to concepts such as common property in Christian tradition, though I'm sure they would not have anticipated its result.

The main concept of poverty flows from the preceding tenet of charity, that a good Christian, loving others as themselves, would share whatever they had with the poor and suffering. You cannot remain in riches if others are starving and consider yourself a good Christian. In the life of Jesus, there was great disparity between the rich and the poor, and many then, as they do today, felt riches could absolve you of sin and make you fit for the Kingdom of God. Jesus explicitly said this is not the case.

*It is easier for a camel to go through the eye of a needle than for a rich man to enter the Kingdom of God.* — Mark 10:25

*... do not store up for yourselves treasures on earth.* — Matthew 6:19

*You cannot serve both God and Money* — Matthew 6:24

*Woe to you who are rich.* — Luke 6:24

His first famous reference to the camel and the eye of the needle is most likely a mistranslation that has been passed down again and again. "Camel" should have probably been translated as "rope," which makes a lot more sense as a metaphor with a needle, though perhaps the image of a camel going through a needle really makes you think about money. Another interpretation is that the reference of "eye of the needle" refers to the smallest entrance to the city of Jerusalem. Only people and small animals could get through it. For a camel to get through it, the animal must bend his legs and head. The fear, confusion, and stubbornness of the animal made it a very difficult process for both the animal and owner.

One of Jesus' most unusual outbursts was when he threw the money lenders out of the Temple. Their presence had become an accepted practice in the Temple but greatly upset Jesus, getting him the closest to violence we see in the official Gospels. Evidently he felt passionate about the separation of money from spiritual matters. It later led to a point of theology preventing Christians from charging interest for loans on any money lent. At first it was to only apply to clergy, but later to all Christians, and led to a point of anti-Semitism, as Jewish people had no such restrictions. While there are some interpretations of Old Testament references against usury, charging interest, it is mostly through references to Jesus in Luke 6:35. *"But love ye your enemy and do good, and lend, hoping for nothing again; and your reward shall be great."* While many see this as an extension of charity and service, others see it directly condemning usury. Today, the mainstream churches for the most part do not condemn the charging of interest as a sin.

## Humility

To be humble is a Christian virtue. Despite his perceived nature, Jesus never really proclaimed himself Lord and demanded worship and tribute. He lived simply. He shared. He did his work and fulfilled his ministry as a teacher. He was not filled with pride and modeled that way of living, claiming his followers would do all that he has done and more.

*The greatest among you will be your servant. For whoever exalts himself will be humbled, and whoever humbles himself will be exalted.* — Matthew 23:11:12

Service is honored among the followers of Jesus rather than those who seek to promote themselves or exalt themselves above others. Earlier in the Gospel of Matthew, Jesus shares with us the message of the child, that to be childlike, without pride and simply be yourself, is the key to the Kingdom of Heaven.

*… the disciples came to Jesus and asked, "Who is the greatest in the kingdom of heaven?" He called a little child and had him stand among them. And he said: "I tell you the truth, unless you change and become like little children, you will never enter the kingdom of heaven. Therefore, whoever humbles himself like this child is the greatest in the kingdom of heaven.* — Matthew 18:1:4

We can encourage our own humility by tapping into our more playful, child-like nature, rather than taking ourselves too seriously and developing a pompous and arrogant attitude. Many of the virtues of Christianity harken back to a younger, more innocent frame of mind, where we simply act as we do and desire harmony with our fellows, without thoughts of revenge, greed, judgment, self-importance and, as demonstrated with the next tenet, sex. The simplicity of a child in day-to-day living opens the gates to this Kingdom of Heaven, our Christ Consciousness.

## Chastity

Another unpopular teaching from Jesus is on sexuality, specifically lust for someone outside of the context of marriage. He mentioned it in this passage:

*But I tell you that anyone who looks at a woman lustfully has already committed adultery with her in his heart. If your right eye causes you to sin, gouge it out and throw it away. It is better for you to lose one part of your body than for your whole body to be thrown into hell. And if your right hand causes you to sin, cut it off and throw it away. It is better for you to lose one part of your body than for your whole body to go into hell.* — Matthew 5:28:30

While he most likely did not mean for anyone to do violence against themselves, he is emphasizing a point. Many have expanded upon this in the dogma of the Church. We have the assumption from early Church fathers that Jesus himself was unmarried and celibate, though Gnostic teachings paint a different portrait of his relationship with Mary Magdalene. If it's true, then the whole theological basis for priests, nuns, and brothers to be unmarried and chaste is on shaky ground.

In other mystical traditions, the concept of periods of celibacy was to focus the energy of consciousness inward for a time. Its sublimation would be channeled through specific rituals and prayers to bring deeper experiences of personal gnosis. It's important to realize most cultures that have such religious teachings have paired them with specific teachings on sexual rituals to be used in other periods. It appears Christianity got the restrictions, but none of the personal, sexual rituals to reach a state of communion with God. Many see it is a conspiracy of the Church to deny the populace and even clergy of an energy of consciousness where they would have direct experience of the divine and thereby no longer need the Church, yet some of the theological concepts are found right here with the words of Jesus, not later from Church fathers, so we're not completely certain if there were more teachings on sexuality he had to offer, if not the populace, to his inner circle.

## Diligence

Diligence is the virtue of hard work, of commitment to the path you have chosen. Jesus realized his path was difficult. While love is what we all seek, not everybody wants to take the actions to create and support love. He said:

*If anyone wishes to come after Me, let him deny himself, and take up his cross, and follow Me.* — Matthew 16:24:26

An interesting allusion to his crucifixion one must imagine was created after his death, but serves to illustrate the difficulty, and sacrifice.

Hard work, by its very name, is hard and not for everybody. While Christianity has been touted as a religion for the masses, for the common man, as it speaks to common issues and ideals, in many ways it takes a remarkable individual to fully and consciously choose it. As we look at the tenets of Christianity and compare it to the history of the Western Church, even up till today, we can see where many of the leaders of the Church cannot fulfill these tenets. How can the common person do so? Through diligent work and trust.

## Trust

Trust is the last of the tenets of the Christian, trust in God, trust in Jesus, and trust in the teachings as leading to a greater consciousness. In times of failing, when we cannot always fulfill these tenets or when we are challenged, to trust that our faith in love and divinity will win out over obstacles, cynicism, and harm from others.

*Do not let your hearts be troubled. Trust in God; trust also in me.* — John 14:1

When you look at these key concepts from the New Testament, it's easy to see a parallel between them and the teachings of the Seven Heavenly Virtues. They are considered the remedies and protections against the Seven Deadly Sins of Christian cosmology, as found in the poem *Psychomachia* by Aurelius Clemens Prudentius in 410 AD. They have their origins in the Pagan writings of Aristotle and Plato, with the four original virtues of Temperance, Wisdom, Justice, and Courage and with the advent of Christianity, the three Theological Virtues of Faith, Hope, and Charity were added to the four Cardinal Virtues. These later morphed into the more common virtues found in Prudentius' work that spread across Europe: Kindness, Temperance, Patience, Charity, Humility, Chastity, and Diligence.

Strange that love is not one of the virtues in either list, but we can see its essence in Kindness. The other tenets, more or less, can be found in one or both of the sets of virtues. The Golden Rule speaks to Temperance. Non-Violence and Forgiveness come from Patience. Charity, Humility, Chastity, and Diligence are self-evident. Poverty comes from the extension of Charity. Trust stems from Faith. Altogether, this paints a good portrait of the tenets of Christianity through Christ's own recorded words.

## Traditional Concepts of Mainstream Christianity

While these ten tenets are key practices for one aspiring to the teachings and example of Christ, we should mention that to be a practicing Christian, there are several more theological points that need to be followed. This is where many mystical Christians and those like me who follow the timeless wisdom traditions truly part ways from the Church. It must be remembered that Jesus Christ was not, despite the name, a Christian. The concept of being a Christian, as a religious identity, came much later. As far as we know, Jesus himself was not specifically founding another religion, but creating a body of teachings, a movement, within Jewish society. One wonders what he might think of the work of his later followers.

The following points are generally accepted by most of the mainstream Christian community, particularly the Catholic Church, as tenets of faith and for some, supersede in action if not word, the instructions left directly by Jesus in the scriptures.

- Belief in One God as the Trinity: God the Father, Jesus Christ as God the Son, and God the Holy Spirit
- Jesus Christ as the Son of God and Messiah
- Salvation from Sin through acceptance of Jesus Christ as Messiah
- Literal death, descent into hell, resurrection, and ascension of Christ
- Belief in the Second Coming of Christ at the Day of Judgement
- Ascension of the Faithful to the Kingdom of Heaven
- Sacredness of the Scriptures

Though many of these concepts are touched upon within the teachings of Jesus, his strongest messages seem simpler than the theology that followed, and he dealt with real world actions one can take to make the world a better place and to treat others with love and dignity.

## Sin, Sacrifice, and Redemption

There is a greater mysticism found in Christianity, beneath the outer appearance of both scripture and dogma. The concept of Christ has evolved over time, from simply meaning the "anointed one", referring to a political liberator, to the messiah, a spiritual savior figure. As the Christian Church sought to absorb many of the various Pagan cults of the time, many other universal themes centered into the Church's doctrine and artwork, particular the Greek and Egyptian mysteries in an effort to win over the Pagan Roman Empire. The earliest expressions of Christianity were more fluid, eclectic, and personal, with contact and influence from other traditions. This period is best seen as Gnostic Christianity, as it emphasized gnosis, a Greek word meaning "knowledge." These Christians sought out direct and divine knowledge from God without an intermediary. Scripture and ritual is a guide, but not a dogmatic structure. Such groups brought together different mystical teachings from the ancient world, and saw Christ as a fulfillment of not only Jewish prophecy, but other esoteric doctrines. The later Christian Church entrenched in its power, sought to convert the rural peasants practicing what would later be called Paganism to the Church by absorbing folk traditions and holidays into the mainstream Christian calendar.

This amalgam of orthodox and somewhat heretical concepts has gone on to fuel the rise of Christian mysticism, growing to new heights of sophistication among Christian esotericists in the Middle Ages. With an influx of material from the Middle East via the Crusades, the arts of alchemy and Cabala flourished in a Christian context beneath the notice of most of the European people. It is in this rich tradition fusing Christianity with ancient Pagan philosophies we see the best tenets of Christian mysticism exemplified as a map for becoming more Christ-like. Like all mystical traditions, it was a personal path, and no one set of philosophies embodied each school, movement, or practitioner, but the collective body of lore from this time informs us on the nature of Christ.

Christ is the savior, but from what is he saving us? Who is he saving? Why? Many good Christians espouse the nature of Christ to save us, but don't ask those questions, or come up with simple answers, like "the Devil." In Christian theology, everyone is considered a sinner. Our concept of sin comes from Jewish tradition, simply meaning "to miss the mark." While it takes that role in Judaism, many other world religions have had similar concepts about mistakes and transgressions translated into English as "sin". It is the Christian traditions that take it to a another level.

Christians, unlike Jews, emphasize the concept of "Original Sin" from the story of creation in the Book of Genesis. While it's an Old Testament story, with parallels in other Middle Eastern mythologies, Christians have a particular interpretation. In the story, after the creation of the world and the first man and woman of the Garden of Eden, Adam and Eve, God gave two commandments: not to eat the fruit of the Tree of Knowledge and not to eat the fruit of the Tree of Life. Eve is tempted by the Serpent to eat an apple from the Tree of Knowledge and suddenly is awoken from her blissful ignorance of the world and urges Adam to eat of it as well. This sin results in the Fall of Mankind, and the banishment of Adam and Eve from paradise.

Rather than simply being the result of the actions of Eve and Adam for disobeying God, it becomes the ancestral sin, the inherited condition of all humanity. We experience an absence of the presence of God and a propensity towards a sinful nature. We exist outside of the state of grace Adam and Eve were born into. Even though we did not personally commit these actions, we bear the consequences of them. We live in this state throughout the "history" of the Old Testament, and that is one of the explanations for why the God of the Old Testament is so authoritarian towards his people. It is through the coming Messiah, the Savior, at least according to Christians, that this attitude will change and a new era will begin. In essence, Jesus is here to save us, to redeem us from our own sinful nature and open the way to heaven.

Jesus as Savior is to fulfill the Jewish prophecy of a messiah, though the Christians ascribed this figure with more mythology than the Jewish people, who still await the messiah. In Christian interpretation, Jesus' main mission beyond the fulfillment of the prophecy, is to make atonement for all of humanity's sins, stemming from our Original Sin and sinful nature. He does this through his suffering and sacrifice and is said to be the last sacrifice needed in the world, for one can be redeemed through faith in Christ and his teachings.

As an aspect of God in the mystery of the trinity, Jesus embodies the concept of the Kingdom of God, or the Kingdom of Heaven, the realm beyond the mortal world, where we could live in God's grace. His presence on Earth was really as an ambassador from this realm to humanity, and to show us the way when he returned to it. Jesus was to defy both death and the Devil, rising from the dead with the promise that the faithful who "receive" him as Savior will also rise from the dead. His promise of everlasting life is sometimes interpreted as those who follow his way are free of the strict Judaic laws of the Old Testament. They will live in the grace of God with Christ. Jesus will establish his kingdom of peace after the end time of this world.

For those of you looking for a more mystical side to the teachings of Christ, the above explanation fits right in with the orthodoxy of most Christian dogma. It's hard to see the timeless wisdom from a tradition that has emphasized that it has the "only way" for everyone. Yet, there is timeless wisdom in these teachings. It started with the Gnostics. The later saints knew it intuitively. The philosophers saw it. The alchemists lived it. And the Cabalists certainly worked with it, and there lies the key to understanding the mystery.

Cabala means "to receive" and refers to a body of mystical teachings on the nature of the divine and various levels of creation. While most strongly associated with Jewish tradition, it might have its origins in the pre-Judiac Pagan religions of the Middle East, or at the very least been highly influenced by Sumerian, Babylonian, and even Egyptian cosmology. Today it is spelled in many different ways and the first letter of the spelling denotes the type of teaching it refers to. Kabalah spelled with a K is most often Jewish teachings. Cabala with a C is usually Christian, or at least Medieval teachings, particularly those of Christian alchemists. Qabalah with a Q refers to magical Qabalah, as occultists adopted many of the ideas from the Cabala, but went beyond the traditional Jewish and Christian associations.

The Cabala is depicted as a "map" through a symbol that has ten circles, known as sephira, meaning "emanations" from the divine, connected with twenty-two lines. Each line is associated with one of the twenty-two letters of the Hebrew alphabet. Together, this diagram of ten circles and twenty-two lines is called the Tree of Life, just like the Tree of Life from the Garden of Eden. Sometimes the back of the tree, its shadow, or an image of it upside down is called the Tree of Knowledge, again like the one in the Garden of Eden. The top of the tree is called Kether or Crown, and is as close to the Divine source as we can comprehend. While Jewish lore depicts the figure associated with Kether as a King, like God the Father, it is said he is in profile, and upon the other side of his "body" is the image of a hidden Queen, showing the divine source as both male and female, hermaphroditic. At the bottom of the tree is Malkuth, the Kingdom, and this is the realm of Earth and humanity. It is seen as the farthest from the source. Its image is a woman or princess, the Holy Sophia, the original title of the Holy Spirit. It is the feminine wisdom throughout the material world, but hidden from view. All the other sephira represent levels of consciousness, dimensions between the extremes of God and man, divinity and mortality.

The problem with most mainstream forms of Christianity is the literal interpretation of what a mystic knows to be an allegory. Many of the outlandish images found in the Bible are not literal truths as most believe, but descriptions of states of consciousness and conditions within the state of the soul as perceived by mystics. When Christian theology is interpreted through this mystical lens, we find strands of the timeless wisdom. The Cabala can open the way to greater understanding of the mysteries of Christ. While eating of the fruit of these trees was forbidden in Eden, they are the means by which we can return back to the Creator.

In the center of the Tree of Life is a level known as Tiphereth. It means beauty, harmony, and even sacrifice. It is associated with the Sun, bright and shining, and can be considered to be the "heart" of the Tree. To Christian Cabalists, Christ is found in Tiphereth, as it is the place of unconditional love and harmony. He is the center of the tree, and you must go "through" him, through his level of consciousness, what some other traditions would call Solar Consciousness, to reach the source of creation. That is what is really meant when Christians say the "way" is through Christ, whether they consciously understand this or not.

In our Tree of Life cosmology, originally Earth, or Malkuth (10-Kingdom), was high on the tree, right beneath the top three sephiroth. In fact, the top three "circles" can be related to Mother Goddess (3-Binah-Understanding), Father God (2-Chokmah-Wisdom), and the supreme Godhead (1-Kether-Crown). Some look at the group as a little family, Mother, Father, Elder, and Daughter. For some reason, the daughter fell from the heights, like a fruit falling from a tree. She became separated from the parents, seemingly lost and distant. Another child, another fruit, was grown in Tiphereth (6-Harmony), the Son, now living somewhere between the parents and the lost Daughter.

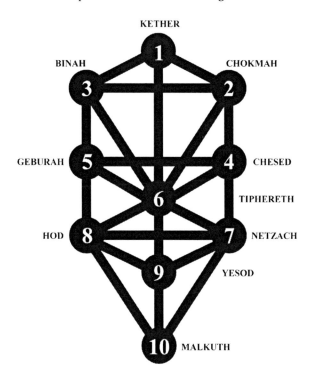

*Figure 5: Traditional Tree of Life*

*Figure 6: Tree of Life with Malkuth Exalted*

The reason for the Fall is found in many mythologies, ranging from the popular story of Eve and Adam eating the fruit, literally picking it off the tree, to rebellious angels falling from grace, to even the sinking of Atlantis. From the most human perspective, it is when humanity developed civilization. We fell out of the animalistic state of harmony with nature, with Eden, and with the invention of language, agriculture and building, we developed concepts of individual identity, personal territory, possessions, and shame. Until that time, like the animals, we didn't know we were "naked in the garden". So that is when we were "forced" to leave it, as once we knew something, we couldn't go back.

Though disturbing, we could see the Fall as a natural part of evolution. Alchemists have a saying, "Dissolve and coagulate." Things constantly need to be broken down, purified, and brought back together in a more perfected state. Our Fall was simply one stage of the work of creation, separation, to bring us back together in an even better, perhaps wiser and more loving, form.

God the Son, the power of Tiphereth, is the bridge between the lowest levels at Malkuth to the highest levels on the Tree. The figure of Jesus, and many other sacrificial figures from mythology, including Tammuz, Dumuzi, Osiris-Horus, Dionysus, Mithras, Balder, and Lleu, descend into the world to act as a bridge between the higher and lower worlds, "rescuing" the Daughter. This is the function of the savior figure. This is the purpose of the redeemer. The Christ figures must open the way. The lower sephira Malkuth and the three above it, Yesod (9), Hod (8), and Netzach (7) represent the terrestrial elements of Earth, Water, Air, and Fire. They must be mastered before you can reach the level of consciousness embodied by the Son/Sun in Tiphereth. Here is where we have the teaching to love God with all your strength, heart, mind, and soul. When you can do that, you can pass through the cloudy veil and reach Christ consciousness. From that point, you better know the higher worlds, God the Mother as well as God the Father, and the source of creation. You are living in the "heart" of the Tree, and the heart of your consciousness, rather than in the belly of consciousness, where desires, safety, and needs rule over love. Living from the heart means all your decisions are heart-based and influence all that you do, even when your basic needs are getting met.

An initiate into any of the ancient or modern mysteries schools learns about the process of death and resurrection in consciousness, and learns to become "Christ-like." Such people know their consciousness is immortal, like the immortality promised by mainstream Christianity. But such mystics know it's not necessarily physical immortality, where physical cadavers will raise up on Judgment Day. We each have our own personal Judgment Day. You can find this in ancient Egyptian mythology, where a soul must go through "negative confessions" of all the things that have not been done, striking a similarity with the Ten Commandments in style and form.

The new world we enter after judgement is the Kingdom of Heaven, as our consciousness will reside in Tiphereth with Christ, and there is no longer a sense of separation, of original sin, to cleave us from the source of creation. We will know eternal love and peace.

Judgment also refers to the changing of the ages, where humanity as a whole will raise their consciousness up the evolutionary ladder. Some will learn to live from this level of Tiphereth, of the heart, while in the body, before death. The Apocalypse is one of the ego, of the limited personality created in the last cycle. So to the personality, it will seem like the world is ending, but it is simply the end of the age, the end of separation, the end of a time where individuality reigns supreme over society and the previous age where society ruled over the needs of the individual. The new age of Tiphereth, where the Daughter and Son, as adults are reunited with the holy family, embodies the paradox of a world where you can be an individual, and still respond to the good of the whole without losing yourself. We will have "sacrificed" what we don't need and what we retain will be transformed. We will be free from the old laws of "thou shalt not" as we will know what is right or wrong in any situation through the connection we have to the divine.

This is what Christ's teaching urge us to do, to be like him, which is the essence of what Christianity is, to be "Christ-like." It's not so much about belief or confession, but following a system of behaviors leading your consciousness to this new level of awareness. All his teachings lead to this direct experience of divinity. Love is the key. Christ is the Son of God, but we too, will all be Daughters and Sons of God. We already are, but need to truly attain Tiphereth consciousness to embody our divinity in the same way. Some mystics see Christ as the example of such a purified human being, showing us the way, though each age has had its avatars of these teachings. Others think of him as the primary bridge, the opener of the way to this consciousness in our age. He is the master-teacher for us at this time and place, so being Christian ostensibly aids you. One could argue that his sacrifice opened the gate, so no one else has to go through such sacrifice and suffering, while others believe you must follow the path, and experience your own personal sacrifice. And if you look at the Tree, you'll notice there are two other ways up the Tree that bypass Tiphereth, so his is not the only way, but the teaching of love in the heart represents the most balanced way to the top of the Tree.

Looking at the Bible through this lens of secret teachings widens our understanding of Christianity from dogmatic religion to timeless wisdom. When we eat of the fruit of the Tree of Knowledge, we can understand the pattern. When we eat of the fruit of the Tree of Life, we rise up the Tree and become immortal like God. A controversial Gnostic teaching tells us the first incarnation of Jesus in the world was the Serpent of the Garden of Eden, which most people mistake for Satan or Lucifer. He "tempts" Eve as he knows we must gain knowledge and thereby wisdom through this hard journey of return. Otherwise, things will stay static and never evolve. This is the secret teaching of Jesus when he tells us to "be ye therefore wise as serpents, and harmless as doves." The serpent is the urge to ascend the tree, found as a totem of wisdom, knowledge, and change all over the world and not necessarily of evil until the outer interpretation of the Bible story, while the dove is the urge to descend down into the world, like the dove of the Holy Spirit.

Now we understand why the Magi of the East were seeking out the King in a stable in Bethlehem. It's much easier to relate Christ to a long chain of teachers and guides throughout history who have a similar message, though he was one of the first to so eloquently put the focus on love, something connected to everyone. Despite the institutions, dogma, politics, and violence that have become part of Christian history, the vision of the Cosmic Christ, and the true purpose of the Savior, is clearer and more accessible to those outside of Christianity who simply seek wisdom.

## The Rituals of Christianity

Like other religious traditions, rituals play a key role beyond the moral, social, and spiritual tenets. Most Christian institutions insist that you need a qualified, consecrated priest or minister to properly administer the rituals to the public. In Catholicism, the main rituals are known as sacraments. According to church theology, they are dispensations of divine life and visible signs of God's grace through the outer celebrations. In those with the proper disposition, they nourish faith. The sacraments are Baptism, Communion, Reconciliation (formerly

Confession), Confirmation, Anointing of the Sick, Holy Orders, and Matrimony. While not everyone receives all of the sacraments in life, they are seen by the Church as necessary steps to salvation and can only be dispensed by the Church.

The early Gnostic gatherings of Christians, however, did not cling to such orthodoxy. Anyone was capable of running rituals. Lots were drawn to determine by "chance,"or the will of God, who would lead. There was more creativity and flow in the rituals, as styles, theology, and philosophy differed amongst the different sects. We can draw from the wisdom of the Gnostic, who sought out direct experience, as we explore the wisdom of this second ray of Christ Consciousness.

The pillars of Christian ritual should be drawn from the actions of Jesus himself, as recorded in the scriptures. These are the actions he models to his apostles and followers. By going back to the accounts, we strip away the accumulated dogma around them and find their simple beauty as a means to connect with Christ's consciousness and unconditional love.

## Prayer

One of the easiest and most accessible ways of performing ritual in a mystical Christian context is prayer. Esoteric circles describe prayer as "speaking" to God while meditation is "listening" to God, in the modern sense of "praying for" things you want to manifest or simply speaking to God about your life in a personal manner, as traditional, ritualistic prayer is very meditative. The repetition of certain phrases ritualistically lends itself to a meditative state of consciousness, like the mantra meditations of repeated sacred phrases found in Hinduism and Buddhism.

One of the most famous Christian prayers is found in the very words of Jesus, the Our Father, or Lord's Prayer, in Matthew 6.

*Our Father, who art in heaven,*
*hallowed be thy name.*
*Thy kingdom come.*
*Thy will be done*

*on earth as it is in heaven.*
*Give us this day our daily bread,*
*and forgive us our trespasses,*
*as we forgive those who trespass against us,*
*and lead us not into temptation,*
*but deliver us from evil.*
*Amen*

Another beloved and popular prayer used mostly in the Catholic tradition of Christianity is the Ave Maria, or Hail Mary, taken from the Gospel of Luke.

*Hail Mary, full of grace. The Lord is with thee.*
*Blessed art thou amongst women,*
*and blessed is the fruit of thy womb, Jesus.*
*Holy Mary, Mother of God,*
*pray for us sinners,*
*now and at the hour of our death.*
*Amen.*

Together the Our Father and Hail Mary make up the core prayers of the Rosary. The Rosary is a beaded tool used to keep count of the prayers, very similar to an eastern tradition using a necklace of 108 beads known as a mala to keep track of mantra repetitions. The formation of the Rosary pattern is circular with five decades, a pattern of ten beads with an additional larger bead before each decade. Connected to the ring is a shorter strand, with a crucifix, larger bead, three smaller beads and larger bead before connecting it to the ring of five decades. Religious orders might use a rosary with fifteen, rather than five decades. Rosaries can be made from any material, but are commonly made from wood, plastic, glass, and stone, as well as semi-precious and precious stones and metals. Rosary beads are not necessary to perform the rosary, and there are other devices of one decade made to help those who pray it keep count, but the ritual of the beads connects one to a long tradition of Christian prayer.

*Figure 7: Rosary Beads*

Begin with the Sign of the Cross, moving your hand from the brow to below the ribs, to the left shoulder and then the right. Eastern Orthodox and Cabalists reverse the horizontal movement, going from right shoulder to left. Then start with the crucifix at the end of the short strand and recite the Apostle's Creed.

> *I believe in God, the Father almighty, creator of heaven and earth.*
> *I believe in Jesus Christ, his only Son, our Lord.*
> *Who was conceived by the power of the Holy Spirit and was born of the*
>   *Virgin Mary.*
> *He suffered under Ponticus Pilate, was crucified, died, and was buried.*
> *He descended into hell. On the third day he rose again.*
> *He ascended into heaven and is seated at the right hand of the Father.*
> *He will come again to judge the living and the dead.*

*Buddha, Christ, Merlin*

*I believe in the Holy Spirit,*
*the Holy Catholic Church, the communion of saints,*
*the forgiveness of sins,*
*the resurrection of the body,*
*and life everlasting.*
*Amen*

Pray the Our Father on the first bead, then three Hail Mary's on the three smaller beads.

Close with the prayer Glory Be to the Father:

*Glory to the Father, and to the Son, and to the Holy Spirit.*
*As it was in the beginning, is now, and will be forever. Amen.*

Pray Our Father on the Large Bead and a Hail Mary on each of the smaller beads. Close with a Glory Be to the Father and repeat the pattern until you complete the line back to the short strand. Conclude with Hail Holy Queen and the Sign of the Cross.

*Hail, holy Queen, Mother of mercy,*
*our life, our sweetness, and our hope.*
*To you we cry, the children of Eve;*
*to you we send up our sighs,*
*mourning and weeping in this land of exile.*
*Turn, then, most gracious advocate,*
*your eyes of mercy toward us;*
*lead us home at last*
*and show us the blessed fruit of your womb, Jesus:*
*O clement, O loving, O sweet Virgin Mary.*
*Amen.*

Throughout Christian history, the use of the Rosary is said to confer healing, blessings, protection, and glory to those who use it, through the intercession of Mary, Jesus' mother. Many who have broken with, or openly defy, the dogmatic institutions of Christianity, still find power, love and wisdom in the recitation of the Rosary. The power of the ritual of it, and the direct connection to St. Mary as Mother of God cannot be underestimated.

The meditation of the Rosary deepens as you develop your understanding. Each of the decades has a Mystery associated with it, to be contemplated. Each is associated with the life of Jesus and Mary. Traditionally there are three sets, though Pope John Paul II added a fourth, known as the Luminous Mysteries. The three traditional mysteries are the Joyful Mysteries of the birth of Jesus, including the Annunciation, Visitation, Nativity, Presentation of Jesus at the Temple, and Finding the lost Jesus in the Temple. The Sorrowful Mysteries involve his agony in the garden, scourging at the pillar, the crown of thorns, carrying the cross, and crucifixion. The Glorious Mysteries are around his resurrection, ascension, the descent of the Holy Spirit, the assumption of Mary into heaven, and the coronation of the Blessed Virgin in heaven.

## Baptism

Christ received Baptism from John the Baptist and in turn baptism has become a staple in Christian rites of passage. Baptism became the first sacrament of the Church. For a Catholic, it is the mark of a Christian. In some denominations of Christianity, including Catholics, it is done with infants, as a rite of passage to enter the body of the Church. In Baptist traditions, it is done with adults, specifically believers. It is in accord with other ceremonial traditions of ritual purification by water and blessing. Pagan traditions did such blessings by rivers as well, and African diasporic traditions continue the process with sacred and floral baths when rivers are not available.

We too can use baptism as a form of ritual rebirth, rededication and purification, regardless of our religious affiliation. There is something universal about the blessings of water in the spiritual journey, not to mention the image of a spiritual rebirth to follow the terrestrial birth. Religious initiations are framed in terms of ritual rebirth. John baptizes people for the forgiveness of sins. Jesus, according to the New Testament, is sinless and does not require it, but is identifying with humanity so closely that he embraces this rite of passage. John the Baptist prophesizes that one will come after him to baptize not only with water, but with fire and the Holy Spirit. Upon Jesus' baptism, the Holy Spirit descends to him in the form of a dove, and he is proclaimed before everyone as the Son of God, fulfilling John's prophecy. Only then does Jesus go out into the wilderness and face temptation.

*Amen, amen I say to thee, unless a man be born again of water and the Holy Ghost, he cannot enter into the kingdom of God.* — John 3:1:21

A simple community ritual of Baptism can be done in small fellowship of Christian mystics. While usually done by a priest or minister, it can be celebrated by any Christian, performed on another. Only two specific parts of the rite are essential. The first is to pour water over the head of the person who is being baptized. In Baptist traditions, the person is fully immersed in water, rather than sprinkled with water. The second part of the rite is the words, "I baptize you in the name of the Father and of the Son and of the Holy Spirit." You can elaborate or adapt the imagery and words to suit your own understanding of Christ and the nature of Baptism.

The washing of Baptism is not unlike the washing of feet found in the Gospel of John 13. Rooted in Middle Eastern hospitality customs, the Gospel of John depicts a scene of Jesus washing the feet of the apostles.

*"If I then, your Lord and Teacher, have washed your feet, you also ought to wash one another's feet. For I have given you an example, that you should do as I have done to you. Most assuredly, I say to you, a servant is not greater than his master; nor is he who is sent greater than he who sent him. If you know these things, blessed are you if you do them."* — John 13: 14:17

Ritual foot washing has been adopted in many Christian denominations, including Roman Catholicism, Eastern Orthodox, and Protestantism. In some traditions it is done by the priest or minister with twelve community members, pouring water over the feet of the twelve, and then drying them. As another ritual of blessings and purification it, too, can be adapted into mystical Christian community rituals.

## Eucharist

The celebration of the Eucharist, the communion of bread and wine, can be considered the primary ritual of Christianity. Though ostensibly drawn from the words and actions of Christ himself at the Last Supper, the origin of the tradition stretches back into Pagan rites where the god of the harvest was honored through cakes, grain, beer, and wine, and ceremonially consumed. One could assume much of the ritual and iconography that made its way into the foundations of the Catholic Church was borrowed from such Pagan traditions, presumably to give the new faith a firmer sense of commonality to attract converts to it.

The basic concept included the consumption of something that had died and been resurrected, more metaphorically in the seasonal change of the harvest, and literally in the transformation of raw ingredients into bread and wine. This conferred similar resurrection properties to those partaking of it. Bread rises, though strangely many Christian mysteries use unleavened bread. Wine has to "die" as the grapes to be reborn as a "spirit." When Christ became more identified with the solar powers and sacrificed god-forms, he gained this mystery. The emphasis of Christianity on resurrection, for Christ and the promise of resurrection for believers, is indicative of this timeless mystery reinterpreted in a new way. The ritual of the sacred meal grants the power of resurrection. In this case, the blessings and grace of Christ by taking his own "body" and "blood" into you.

The term Eucharist actually means "thanksgiving" in Greek, as Christ gives "thanks" in the Last Supper. It is also known as Holy Communion, as communion refers to participation, fellowship or partaking. Saint Paul's first letter to the Corinthians has the earliest depiction of the Last Supper.

*For I have received of the Lord that which also I delivered unto you, that the Lord Jesus the same night in which he was betrayed took bread: And when he had given thanks, he brake it, and said, Take, eat—this is my body, which is broken for you—this do in remembrance of me. After the same manner also he took the cup, when he had supped, saying, this cup is the new testament in my blood: this do ye, as oft as ye drink it, in remembrance of me. For as often as ye*

*eat this bread, and drink this cup, ye do shew the Lord's death till he come.* — I
Corinthians 11:23–26

In the Catholic liturgy, the "host", or unleavened bread, is
administered with the words "This is my body" while the wine is
administered with "this is my blood." Catholics believe in the mystery of
Transubstantiation of the bread and wine into the literal flesh and blood
of Christ, despite what all the senses indicate as merely bread and wine.
From this perspective, the bread and wine are literally absent and, in its
place, the flesh and blood of Christ is now present. Catholics believe in
this literally, not symbolically. The remaining hosts in the tabernacle are
honored and genuflected towards to acknowledge the literal presence of
Christ's body within the tabernacle. Consumption of the host is said to
confer the transmission of Christ's grace upon the receiver. Most other
traditions see the materials blessed or consecrated with the divine grace
of Christ, or perhaps the presence of Christ within or beneath the outer
form of wine and bread, but Catholics believe in a literal transformation
of the material. Protestants don't see the ritual so much as a channel for
divine grace, but a sign of belief. It is done in memory of Christ's actions
at the Last Supper, where he not only shared bread and wine, but
revealed that one of the apostles would betray him.

Jesus' "New Testament", commemorated in this ritual act, and sealed
with his crucifixion, is the idea that Jesus is the last religious sacrifice. His
death and resurrection for the sins of all people are to redeem everyone,
not just those alive at that time, but past, present, and future. The pacts
of the Old Testament and the harsher vision of God is replaced with this
new promise, given by the Son of God to his people.

The spirit of the ritual, outside of the official sanction of various
Christian Churches, can be performed by believers both wishing to
receive the grace of Christ directly, and to remember his ministry and
sacrifice. Many traditions before and after Christ's time have used the
ritual meal of wine and bread. I'm most familiar with it through the
ritual of the Mystical Repast, from the magical tradition of the Golden
Dawn. While embodying many Christian principles, the meal is similar
in form, if not meaning, to the Eucharist. I find it interesting to speak to

so many healers, mystics, and magicians with strong Christian leanings, either from childhood or beyond, who would "play" the Eucharist with bread and juice, and have no idea why the adults were mad at them for doing it, as it seemed natural. As we recapture that childlike quality that Christ encouraged, we reclaim the power to hold ceremony for ourselves, and receive grace from the Divine directly.

The ritual of the Eucharist can be preceded by the Our Father, or any other prayer deemed appropriate to set the sacred space and prepare you for communion. The following ritual is adapted from the Catholic Mass. The bread can be placed on any special, ritual plate and the wine into any ritual cup or chalice.

### Blessing of the Bread and Wine

*Blessed are you, Lord, God of all creation. Through your goodness we have this bread to offer, which earth has given and human hands have made. It will become for us the bread of life. Blessed be God forever.*

*Blessed are you, Lord, God of all creation. Through your goodness we have this wine to offer, fruit of the vine and work of human hands. It will become our spiritual drink. Blessed be God forever.*

*May the Lord accept the sacrifice at our hands, for the praise and glory of His name, for our good, and the good of all the world.*

### Heartfelt Prayer over the Bread and Wine

(also known as the *Proclaiming of the Mystery of Faith*)
*Christ has died, Christ is risen, Christ will come again.*
*Lord's Prayer (If not already recited)*

### Breaking of the Bread with the words:

*Lamb of God, you take away the sins of the world—have mercy on us.*
*Lamb of God, you take away the sins of the world—have mercy on us.*
*Lamb of God, you take away the sins of the world—grant us peace.*

*This is the Lamb of God who takes away the sins of the world. Happy are those who are called to his supper. Lord, I am not worthy to receive you, but only say the word and I shall be healed.*

*The body of Christ. Amen. (Consumption of the Bread) The blood of Christ. Amen. (Consumption of the Wine)*

*Silent Prayer and Communion with the Divine.*

## Healing

Healing was a staple of Jesus' ministry upon Earth. He was well known for his miracles of healing the sick, as each was an example of his divine presence to correct illness within an individual and return them to perfection. To the later Christians, healing was part of Jesus' mission of forgiveness, and there is a sense of illness being tied together with a sense of sin. When the sin was forgiven by Jesus' divine presence, the illness was cured. While many of a Christian background look at such healing as exclusive to Jesus as the Son of God, he said that his followers would do all the he has done and more, and his healing work sometimes bore a strong resemblance to the healing work of the holy men of other cultures, the shamans and gurus, who would cast out demons and restore vitality. Even his use of mud and spit to cure blindness smacks of a form of folk magic.

*And as Jesus passed by, he saw a man which was blind from his birth. And his disciples asked him, saying, Master, who did sin, this man, or his parents, that he was born blind? Jesus answered, Neither hath this man sinned, nor his parents: but that the works of God should be made manifest in him. I must work the works of him that sent me, while it is day: the night cometh, when no man can work. As long as I am in the world, I am the light of the world. When he had thus spoken, he spat on the ground, and made clay of the spittle, and he anointed the eyes of the blind man with the clay, And said unto him, Go, wash in the pool of Siloam, (which is by interpretation, Sent.) He went his way therefore, and washed, and came seeing. The neighbors therefore, and they which before had seen him that he was blind, said, Is not this he that sat and begged? Some said, This is he: others said, He is like him: but he said, I am he. Therefore said they unto him, How were thine eyes opened? He answered and said, A man that is called Jesus made clay, and anointed mine eyes, and said unto me, Go to the pool of Siloam, and wash: and I went and washed, and I received sight. Then said they unto him, Where is he? He said, I know not.* — John 9: 1:12

Throughout the Christian tradition, and even today, miraculous healing has been attributed to saints and preachers, leading to a tradition of "faith healing" and "laying on of hands" similar to other spiritual traditions, with the crucial difference that the faith be oriented towards Christ, and its God the Father, through Christ, who bestows the grace and forgiveness of healing. Such faith healing is similar to the energy healing of other traditions, techniques that restore the vital life force to the body, and require no specific belief system from either/both the recipient or healer. Today Christians seeking to emulate the healing of Jesus are involved in a variety of religious and mystical traditions of healing. The most conservative Catholic sacrament is the Anointing of the Sick. Some compare Eastern techniques of healing, such as the Japanese system of Reiki, to the ministry of Christ, particularly to open the minds of conservative Christians to the teachings of Reiki.

A simple ritual modern mystical Christians can perform is anointing the sick with oil for healing. Though traditionally done by a priest in the Catholic faith, as it is thought to forgive sins much like the sacrament of Reconciliation, in the spirit of the Gnostic Christians, anyone can do it. In the past it has usually been done for physical ailments, particularly those close to death due to its older title, Extreme Unction, but now, in less traditional settings, can be used to bring healing to any situation, emotional, mental, or spiritual.

Olive oil can be blessed by the one performing this ritual with an appropriate prayer. Usually the brow is anointed with the sign of the cross and the words:

*Through this holy anointing, may the Lord in his love and mercy help you with the grace of the Holy Spirit.*

The hands are anointed with oil and then the words:

*May the Lord who frees you from sin save you and raise you up.*

Then specifically ill parts of the body can be anointed. Older forms of the rite anointed seven parts of the body, relating to the seven "senses" of sight, hearing, smell, taste, touch, walking, and carnal delectation, with the sins of each associated sense being forgiven.

Hopefully the underlying themes of Christianity, and the historic rites associated with it, can be assimilated into a new Christian context free from binding dogma and allowing the light and love of the Christ to shine through in its experiences.

# Chapter Nine: The Way of Magic

Merlin has no religion named after him. There is no "Merlinism," much to the disappointment of many fans of Arthurian mythology looking for a religion. In fact, it's often unclear what religion, if any, he practiced. Most of us think of him as a Pagan priest, a Druid, or shaman. Yet other tales depict him almost entirely devoid of British Paganism and the Goddess of the Land. These stories show him squarely in the Christian world, trying to redeem his darker and lecherous nature by working against the influence of the Christian Devil for the favor of God the Father and his son Jesus.

Merlin certainly didn't seem to espouse a dogma or philosophy for all to follow. Though he was a prophet, he predicted the future, and how the past would influence the world. He didn't proselytize to convert people to any one faith. He gave counsel, but ultimately the decisions were up to others. While various books are attributed to him, or about him, none clearly describe his beliefs. There is no true historic *Book of Merlin* clearly depicting his philosophy, only collections of poems and prophecies attributed to him. Monmouth's *Prophecies of Merlin* and *Life of Merlin* are the closest we have, and perhaps they have coded information found in folkloric material, but they are not a clear "how to" manual for those aspiring to the path of Merlin. Merlin's function seems to be advising and encouraging others to action, and aiding where he can. Whether you went to church in the stone building with the priest or to the forest with the trees did not matter as long as you did what was necessary.

He seemed entirely comfortable in a world where the principles of British Paganism were merging and blending with Christian belief. He seemed at home in the realms "between", having a foot in both worlds, yet really belonging to neither. That is the hallmark of a shaman. Shamans are "walkers between the worlds" having one foot in the realm of humanity, the village or tribe, and another in the community of spirits, gods, and ancestors. The shaman forms the bridge between the two.

His native Britain has always been a melting pot for religious mysteries. Starting with the various waves of Stone Age people who were the builders of the megaliths and stone circles, followed by the historic invasions from the east by the Indo-Europeans such as the Celts, to the mythic settlements from the West from fabled sunken cities. The invasion of Rome brought Roman beliefs, temples, and culture to parts of England, and shortly after their withdrawal came the Saxons. Each of these peoples has rich philosophies, beliefs, and magic that has melded together in the British Isles.

Merlin is a magician. Magic is his vocation, his way of life. He could also be considered a Wizard or Witch for, in many ways, those are magical vocations. Almost any priest or prophet of the ancient world could be called a magician – such as Moses, Enoch, Zarathustra, Orpheus, Lao Tsu, even Buddha and Christ – his way is the epitome of magic, where for others, magic was just a tool in their own mission, an ancient science to be applied to a situation, just as chemistry or engineering would be used today. Not so for Merlin.

Merlin's whole life was a manifestation of magic. It was a manifestation of what magicians call the "Great Work." The Great Work is the magician's quest for enlightenment and union with "God", the creative force, through understanding and participating in Nature. But what is magic? Magicians and philosophers have spent a great deal of time trying to define exactly what magic is and, much like arguments over pornography, while we might not all agree on the definition, we all know it when we see it.

## Defining Magic

One of the more commonly accepted definitions of magic is from a controversial modern magician named Aleister Crowley. His name, rhyming with "holy", is often mispronounced, and he did consider his work "holy" and for the betterment of humanity, despite the mischief and negative press he encouraged. His actions were typically veiled in secrecy and misunderstanding, much like Merlin, and in many ways could be seen as an incarnation of the Merlin figure in the twentieth century.

Crowley saw himself as a prophet as well, and espoused the virtues of his new magical religion, called Thelema, which means "Will" in Greek. He considered Thelema the new magical religion of the next age or "aeon" as he called it. He believed the old dogmatic religions had outlived their usefulness. The next age is one of magic and we all need to know how to be magicians to live in it. He even spelled magic differently, with a "k" at the end, to distinguish stage show slight of hand *magic* from the royal art and science of *magick*.

His definition of magic is "the science and art of causing change to occur in conformity with the Will." Basically it means a person can have an intention and, through an act of will, change reality to conform to that intention. By Crowley's definition, any intentional change, occult or not, is an act of magic.

If I decide it is my will that the vase within my room be to my left, and not to my right, and I get up and put the vase on the left side of the room, that was magic. Crowley included banking, potato growing, and blowing your nose as all forms of magic by his definition. But more often than not, most people are referring to less mundane manifestations of will, acts of ritual magic and spell casting.

The act of will can be pure energy, pure intent, but for most people, the actions of a ritual help express the energy of the desire and are more likely to manifest the desire. A more esoteric expression of magic would be to perform a ceremony for a new job, and then, a few hours later, get a call from a friend who knows about a position that would be perfect for you. You interview and are offered the job. Magic!

Magic typically manifests through what appears to be coincidence. It's easy to dismiss. At least at first it's very easy to dismiss. But when you live a magical life, you live a life of a never ending series of coincidences and synchronicities, and realize that "coincidence" indicates some greater unseen force at work. Even if you don't understand exactly how, or have a spiritual framework to put it into perspective, you know it works, and continue to use the principles you know.

It might sound strange, but some of the best magicians out there have no idea they are magicians. The principles of magic are used by successful people in all walks of life. Some of the most powerful magicians I know are either business executive types or artists and musicians. Each has a will, a vision or intention, and each has worked to manifest it. While anyone can have success, the quality of success that occurs with magic seems almost supernatural.

To the magician, magic is not supernatural in the sense of being unnatural or outside of nature. It is a wholly natural force. It cannot break the laws of the cosmos, but it seemingly bends them. While I don't know too many magical people who can shoot lighting from their fingertips like in some movie or novel, I've known magical people to walk away unharmed from deadly accidents that baffled rescue workers. I've known people to be in the most perfect spot to get an opportunity offered that would fulfill their dreams. But part of the magic is having the wisdom to take action when those opportunities are presented.

Magic is science because there are specific principles governing its operation. Material science is just catching up to some of the principles, expressing them in terms of quantum physics. While it might seem foolish to some, with no proof, think about all the fundamental forces that have been around us all throughout history that we are just learning to conceptualize, measure, and express. Gravity has always affected us, even though it took Sir Isaac Newton to theorize and "prove" its law in 1687. The experience of gravity predated 1687, but we didn't have a clear name for it. The principles of magic are the same way. The ancient arts and philosophies were creatively expressing these principles to the best of their ability.

The creative expression of magic is the art of magic. Once you understand the underlying principles, you can be artistic in the manner in which you use them. Rituals and ceremonies are filled with great beauty. They can all be very different and potentially equally effective. Magical religions and traditions of healing are based upon the same fundamental principles, but each culture expresses them differently, adding the artistic worldview of their people, place, and time period. The land where you live and the time in which you live shapes both your art and religion as each influences the access you have to materials, time, and information.

## Will

An important part of Crowley's definition of magic is the word "will." We think of will as desire, as our wants, and that is one interpretation of the word. My own magical teacher challenged me one day. While reviewing the ethical teaching known as the *Wiccan Rede,* summed up as "And it harm none, do as ye will," I had a teacher challenge me to spell will. Of course I answered "w-i-l-l". She asked me again. And again I repeated "w-i-l-l". She was obviously not satisfied, and then asked me if the W was lower case or capitol? I did not understand. My teacher then proceeded to tell me that while it is usually written as a lower case "w" such writings were often in error. Will with a lower case "w" indicates your lower will, the desires of your personality and ego. They are not considered bad by magicians and Witches. On the contrary, they are holy because they can lead you to your Will with a capitol "W". Will with a capitol "W" is the True Will, the Divine Will, the Mystic's Will. There are many names for it. It is the Will of your soul. It is the purpose you are here to fulfill over the course of a lifetime and in any given moment. To live your life in fulfillment of this Will is the Great Work. It transforms you and brings you close to the divine.

Magicians sometimes divide magic along the artificial divide of "low" magic and "high" magic. Low magic is aimed at fulfilling your desires. It is what most people without a lot of experience on the path of magic think of when they think of magic. People think how wonderful a magician's life must always be because they can get anything they want at anytime.

High magic is any magic involving aligning with your soul and purpose, often it has no tangible or immediate effect. High magic is considered "God-Magic" as it brings you closer to the divine. High magic is considered spiritual and for the benefit of your evolution. All of this is true, yet the same could be said about low magic.

When you explore any magic, it is best to do so in the spirit that the magic be "for the highest good, harming none." When we hold onto that intention, regardless of whether the magic would be considered "low" or "high", we transform the magic. It all becomes God-Magic. If the intention is for the highest good and it manifests, it is pointing you towards actions in harmony with your soul's purpose.

If the intention is ultimately not for your good, or would harm others, the magic fails, and shows you what is out of harmony with your soul, and will result in an imbalance if you pursue it. If you really desire it, the magic gives you the opportunity to reflect on that desire, understand its origin, and perhaps resolve it, either by making the "mistake" of getting it, or learning how to let go without manifesting it.

The work of magic is much like the fabled tales of genies granting three wishes. We say, "Be careful what you wish for, because you just might get it." Others say, "May the gods grant me what I need and protect me from what I want." Sometimes the magic comes in getting what you thought you wanted, only to find that the result wasn't at all what you thought it would be.

You can only use the success and failure of your magic as a guide to your True Will if you are performing all your magic with the intention that it be for "the highest good" or "in accord with divine will" and if you have sufficient knowledge and skill to perform magic successfully. Like any art and science, it requires knowledge, practice and preparation. Only when you have a strong foundation does the magic becomes a more reliable guide on the path to find and manifest your True Will.

If we look at the stories of Camelot, we see a wide range of exploration of will and desire. When the king is acting in accord only with the lower will, the world suffers. Vortigern's tower, built for reasons of fear rather than leadership, collapses continually. But his selfish desire and willingness to sacrifice an innocent starts Merlin's own journey as a prophet and magician. Uther's desire for Ygraine does have a higher purpose, yet Uther was not one to manifest True Will, so Merlin had to work with Uther's lower will, his simple desires, to move the land closer to harmony and arrange the birth of Arthur.

The common story of Lancelot and Gwenievere's betrayal, and in particular Arthur's reaction to it, results in the lower will, not the higher. But with that destruction came the quest for the Holy Grail, and the opportunity for greater healing of the land and its people, and the exploration of a deeper mystery. We sometimes need to feel separation from divinity, and the divine land, to purify, heal, and return with greater wisdom. Alchemists say we must "separate the subtle from the gross" meaning we must purify. Only then can we return.

Merlin's apprentice, whose desire for power and Merlin's own desire for companionship, love, or even sex, led to his own imprisonment. Yet, did those desires lead to a higher purpose? Without them, would Merlin undergo imprisonment and transformation? Would his wisdom be accessible to us as it is today, unlike any other magician in the ancient world? His otherworldly imprisonment really led to his ascension and immortality in the hearts and minds of humanity. There he can do much more good with us as teacher and guide, instead of walking the Earth in another body, limited to one physical location and time and thereby limiting his aid.

We never know where our desire will lead us. We never truly know the results of our magic. While these stories don't always show our human desire in the best of light, as there can be "better" ways for it to be expressed, we can see the theme of Higher Will interwoven with all the expression of the lower will, urging us onward. Desires in and of themselves are holy.

In the western magical traditions, particularly in the arts of alchemy where philosophers were transforming lead into gold, there is a phrase: "Dissolve and coagulate." Things must be broken apart, dissolved, seemingly destroyed to be purified and rejoined again. Our faults, our failings, our "sins" lead us into the dark night of the soul, which is ultimately a healing and rejuvenating experience for those who can navigate it. The magician, like the figures of Buddha and Christ, must descend into the underworld, the dark forest, to "hell" and return.

Darkness and destruction serve a purpose. If everything was perfect already, and there was no separation, there would be no creativity. There would be no development, evolution, or innovation. There would be no purpose to life, time and space. Our imperfections give us the opportunities, to explore, invent, and recreate ourselves and the world in harmony with the divine. We are part of the creative principle. That is the essence of magic. That is the secret to healing our personal and collective wounds. The sacred wound of the King, and its healing through the Grail, is a central part of the Arthurian mythos.

## Communication

While magic is usually thought of as action, an expression of will, higher or lower, there is another part to it that is sometimes forgotten. Magic is communication. It is the expression of your will to the divine, but also listening back to the divine's response. To have true communication, both sides need to have the ability to listen and to speak. A good magician does not have a one-sided conversation with the divine. If he does, soon that magic becomes unfulfilling and empty.

Some say prayer is speaking to God, while meditation is listening to God. Magic is both. The active side of magic, akin to prayer, is made up of the rituals, ceremonies, and spells that help communicate your intention to the universe. A ritual or spell is just a symbolic action with the necessary energy to communicate your intention to the divine. Spells are copied in spell books and repeated because they work. Once a particular ritual action is successfully recognized by the divine, it becomes easier for those who repeat it. Spells that are repeated over time seem more powerful because that channel of communication already exists. Such spells are usually for the basics of life, as all people have the same basic human needs. New spells can be more difficult, but more rewarding, as they are tailored to your specific needs at the time.

The receptive side of magic is psychic ability. While you might think of psychic ability as a separate gift, it's really the other side to the "coin" of ritual. Many who are talented with ritual magic don't explore the psychic side, while many who are naturally psychic don't seek out magical ritual. But unless you have both, it's like you are working with one hand tied behind your back.

To be psychic simply means to listen to your psyche. Today we think of our psyche as the mind, yet the ancient use of the word was much closer to the concept of soul, or at least part of your soul. To be psychic really means to communicate with your soul. Through it, you have access to all sorts of information.

Merlin is described as a prophet. What actually defines one as a prophet? In this context, it meant he was a "seer", someone with psychic perception. Seer implies psychic sight, what we call clairvoyance, though a prophet might receive information as visions, a voice (called clairaudience), or simply a sense of knowing without words or pictures (clairsentience). Many times the bards of the Celtic traditions would have the words of their prophecies roll off the tongue and would have no idea what they were going to say until they said it. Such magicians were said to have the "tongue that cannot lie" and it's unclear if their prophecies were proclamations or psychic predictions. Did the very fact they said it make it an act of magic, a ritual to manifest divine intent through declaration, or were they psychically receiving information of what was to come? From the deepest levels of magic, when you are aligned with Will, there is no difference between the two, they are two sides of the same power.

Merlin's visions guidef him. In a sense, they were spells – declarations of what would be from the divine. In another, they were roadmaps, helping inform his actions to bring about his visions. Some required no work on his part. They were simply present, like the dragons under the tower. He didn't need to make them. They already existed. But we can only assume some of the more unusual parts of his myth were guided by his visions – the conception of Arthur, the sword in the stone, Excalibur and the Lady of the Lake, the building of Camelot and the crafting of the Round table. Why would he take such unusual and outlandish actions unless he was fulfilling his Higher Will in the larger scheme of things, as he saw it, and helping others find their Higher Will and express it in the world? He could only do his part, to the best of his ability at the time, just as all the other players in the Arthurian cycle.

**Consciousness**

Consciousness is a huge part of magic. Without awareness, without conscious action and conscious perception, there is no magic. While some low magic can seem to occur without clear conscious intent, it doesn't lead to True Will in the same way a fully engaged and conscious magician does.

Dion Fortune added to the definition of magic, saying that magic was "causing change in consciousness to occur," because the first change to occur has to be in your own consciousness. When you can both perform ritual and "listen" for its results within you, you are well on your way to becoming a true magician.

Fortune's words imply that if you cannot make an internal change in harmony with your will, you will never be able to make an external change. Rituals and spells first change you, and through that change, you are able to manifest what you desire. If you cannot feel love for yourself, no manner of spell will help attract a lover. The ritual's purpose is to help you feel the love you want to attract, even for an instant and broadcast that instant out to the universe. In that instant, you've created a change in your consciousness. Hopefully the change is more long-lasting, but once you've experienced something internally, you can manifest it externally. Magicians believe one world is the reflection of the other, "As above, So below". Mirrors and still pools of water are the symbol of the separation between the "normal" and magical worlds.

# The Way of Magic

Magic can be seen as a way of life and there are specific principles and practices that go into making a magical life. By our own exploration of magic, the concepts of will, consciousness, and communication are key. Another way to put it is what are referred to as the three requirements of magic:

1. Strength of Will
2. Clear Intention
3. Method of Energy Direction

The first is strength of will. It can be the strength of desire, of the lower will, or the strength of the higher will, but if there is no will involved on any level, it is difficult to do magic.

Clear intention is the second component, jointly with the first. Neither really can come before the other, but both are needed. You can be willful but unclear about what you want. You can have an image of a potential creation and still have no real will or energy to manifest it. Magic only works when you conjoin will with intention.

The last of the three is a method to direct the energy of your will and intention. Ritual is the process through which we generate, gather, and direct energy for our purposes. When you know what you are doing, ritual is removed from the realm of superstition and becomes an organic technology, natural to the human experience. We use repeated actions all the time to communicate things to ourselves, to each other and, through magic, to the divine. Rituals are a method to stoke our emotions, an "energy-in-motion", to fuel our magic. The intensity of rituals, even simple rituals, help evoke emotions, in a controlled and measured way, and gives us a method to direct those emotions. The best rituals are those that inspire a sense of love, wisdom, and awe of the divine. Think of any moving ceremony you've attended – a wedding, funeral, or graduation. Have you had any particularly inspiring religious experiences? Even though I'm no longer Catholic, there is something very moving about a High Mass performed by an inspired priest. Think of the words of a song, poem, play, or movie. All of these provide a stimulus to release genuine emotion. They generate, build up, and have release, often with a message. They are forms of ritual. The only difference between them and magic is the magical ritual will direct those released emotions towards a specific goal.

Rituals can be elaborate, with things like candles, incense, oils, and herbs, or as simple as a focused visualization or spoken word. But the ritual method has to be able to focus and send out energy to the universe. Without it, it is like having a great idea and the desire to make it real, but no ability to speak or draw to express it to another person and get the help you need. The energies of desire and intention not directed toward their goal, can at the least, wither away the intention, and at worst, go corrupt and create an obsession.

Some magicians are more verbal and like to express their ritual in words, spoken or thought. These spells are like speaking to the universe directly. Others are more symbolic, and do better with ritual actions and working with objects from nature in harmony with the intent; they are like drawing a picture for the universe. Both work. It just depends on the magician.

## The Principles of Magic Rituals

All acts of magic are rituals, even though they might not appear to be. "Ritual" is a word that can scare people. They believe it involves something harmful. It doesn't. That fear stems from our concept of the taboo. Something is taboo when it is both sacred and profane. It is something not for the masses. Only particular people are called to work with the taboo. Since these ideas and actions are apparently "forbidden" by the mainstream world, crossing the line into the taboo generates a tremendous amount of energy for magic. Many religious initiation ceremonies in the traditions of magic, Druidry, Freemasonry, and Wicca are kept secret and taboo, mysteries, to evoke that response in the student. Yet, according to Crowley, we are entering an age where we all have to be familiar with magic, to be budding magicians, and cross the line into what was once taboo.

When you understand the process of magical rituals, it doesn't make them any less mysterious and moving, but it can remove some of the fear associated with them. Magical rituals have some basic concepts found in many, if not all, traditions. They include: Sacred Space and Time, the Four Powers, Symbolism, Correspondence, and the Moon.

## Sacred Space and Time

Rituals mark a boundary of not only space, but also time. Magicians are said to enter a point of timelessness, beyond ordinary space and time. If you enter a state of deep meditation and contemplation, which can occur not only in a spiritual context, but daydreaming or driving to work, you lose all sense of time and place. You have entered a time beyond. Magicians do the same thing, but control the shift and remain conscious while doing so. Sacred space and time are marked by opening and closing rituals, to start and end the work. They involve the marking of a real or imaginary (energetic) circle. Medieval magicians would mark the circle with chalk or salt on the floor, white for purification. Witches would mark the circle in twigs, flowers, or by dancing. Many ancient sacred sites around the world are marked by a circle of stones, such as the Native American medicine wheels. Usually ceremonies to create or manifest are performed "sun-wise." In the Northern Hemisphere it would be clockwise and in the Southern Hemisphere, counterclockwise. Deosil (correctly pronounced *jeshil* or *jedsil*) is a popular Gaelic term for sun-wise.

## The Four Powers

The rituals of opening and closing are supplemented by a ceremonial acknowledgement of the four powers. Four is the number of manifestation in the material world and the square is its symbol. Esoteric philosophy says everything in the world has four components – a spiritual force, a mental force, an astral or emotional force, and a physical result. Such powers have been described in the west as the classic four elements: fire, air, water, and earth. With modern science, "element" is a confusing term, as they are not the elements of the periodic table like hydrogen or nitrogen. The classical four elements are four qualities: transformation, space, flow, and solidity. Modern practitioners equate them with the scientific principles of electromagnetism, strong nuclear force, weak nuclear force and gravity, or the four sequences found in DNA molecules. The ancient peoples were more poetic in their understanding, equating them with the four directions, the four winds, or four creatures said to hold up the world. In *The Bible*, they are found in the Old Testament vision of Ezekiel, as the lion, man, eagle, and bull. They correspond with the fixed Zodiac signs of Leo, Aquarius, Scorpio, and Taurus, respectively. Modern magicians see them as Light, Life, Love, and Law. Judeo-Christian magicians associate them with the archangels Michael, Raphael, Gabriel, and Uriel. They are also associated with the apostles Matthew, Mark, Luke, and John. Any act of magic uses these four powers, consciously or unconsciously. Simply acknowledging the four directions in a sun-wise motion is sufficient. Most modern traditions assign earth to the north, air to the east, fire to the south, and water to the west.

## Symbolism

Ritual is based upon symbolism, as this is the best method to speak clearly to the universe. We are thinking creatures, with an extensive internal dialogue and, for some, an extensive external dialogue. We process our feelings and experiences through thoughts and words, and don't often put our full will (or Will) behind our words. It can be difficult for the universe to know when we are making a magical declaration and when we are simply talking with no desire for results. Even when we do, our words can be ambiguous at best and sometimes magic gives you exactly what you asked for, not what you meant. When you do a spell for a new job, and that's all you ask, you might get a new, lower paying job by being demoted. Not exactly what you thought you intended. Symbols are a traditional way we speak to the intelligence of Nature and the Universe about our intention. When we ritualistically perform actions representing what we want, or when we speak in a direct and ritualized format, we speak more clearly. A simple act of symbolism involves magic to make it rain during a draught. By pouring water through a sieve or colander during a ritual, you are showing the divine intelligence, including the part of divine intelligence that resides within you, exactly what you want: The sprinkling of rain. A ritual to bring people closer together might involve moving two dolls closer together. A spell to remove illness could involve writing the name of the illness on a slip of paper and then dissolving it in water and flushing it down the toilet. Money magic can involve images of dollar signs or mock checks for the amount you want. The classic technique of symbolism in the modern age is to visualize exactly what you want, the end result of your intention. Picture yourself as already accomplished with the result. This sends the clearest signal to the universe about your intention, and is the heart of the much vaunted "Secret" of occult traditions and modern New Age movements.

## Correspondence

Correspondence is similar to symbolism, but a less well-known principle. While we all use symbols in our daily life, including the letters of the alphabet to speak and spell, correspondence involves the very nature of the universe and the world around us. The Principle of Correspondence states, "As above, so below. As within, so without." It is the building block of alchemy, Hermeticism, and all magic. Basically it means everything in the heavens, the starry sky, and even the unseen spiritual realms, has a correspondence to something in the material realm, from the world around us to the world within us, within our bodies. Magic is a process of using these correspondences to align with the forces we desire.

For example, in the solar system, we have the planet Venus. In the immaterial realm, Venus corresponds with love, relationships, and the power of attraction. She is described as the Goddess of Love in Greek myth. In our personal life, this manifests as our romances, marriages, and friendships. In the world around us, there are various items spiritually corresponding to Venus, including the plants rose, yarrow, and lady's mantle, the stones emerald, rose quartz, and kunzite, the metal copper, the day Friday, and the color green. Each of these things is said to have a similar vibration to the powers of Venus. If you are on a piano, it's like each one is the note F, but in a different octave. They sound similar, but are not exactly the same. Yet when you hold the pedal on the piano down and hit just one F anywhere on the keyboard, all the F's resonate. They correspond. So if you want to bring the power of Venus into your magic, perform the ritual on Friday, wear the color green, carry an emerald, and wear rose oil. Each of these helps you connect with this divine force, and through symbolism and declaration, you can clearly state your will.

| PLANET | INTENTIONS | DAY | COLOR | METAL | STONES | PLANTS |
|---|---|---|---|---|---|---|
| Sun | Success, Health | Sunday | Yellow | Gold | Citrine, Pyrite | Sunflower, St John's Wort, Rosemary |
| Moon | Intuition, Family | Monday | Purple | Silver | Moonstone, Beryl | Mugwort, Jasmine, Camphor |
| Mars | Will, Protection | Tuesday | Red | Iron | Ruby, Garnet | Nettles, Pepper, Thistle, Parsley |
| Mercury | Memory, Travel | Wednesday | Orange | Quicksilver | Agate, Carnelian | Scullcap, Dill, Valerian |
| Jupiter | Good Fortune, Success | Thursday | Blue | Tin | Turquoise, Lapis | Cinnamon, Lemon Balm |
| Venus | Love, Attractions | Friday | Green | Copper | Rose quartz, Emerald | Rose, Yarrow, Lady's Mantle |
| Saturn | Protection, Binding | Saturday | Black | Lead | Jet, Onyx | Horsetail, Comfrey, Mandrake |

## The Moon

The Moon is the last important aspect of magic, though not all magicians follow its guidance. As the closest heavenly body to the Earth, it is said to be the gateway to the higher powers and to "rule" or influence the work of all magic. Just as each of the days of the week have an influence on us, so does the cycle of the Moon. The general guideline is when the Moon is growing in light, or waxing, as it heads towards being full, it is a time for magic to increase things or gain what you want. When the Moon is waning, or diminishing in light, as it heads towards being new, it is a time to decrease things, remove obstacles or banish unwanted forces. While knowledge of the Moon is a great guide, and following it can promote balance and awareness in the cycles of Nature, not all traditions follow it. Some are more focused on the timing of the Sun or stars. You can find more information about the Moon's waxing and waning from an astrological calendar or almanac, or various online Moon calendars.

## Making Magic

Now that you understand the basics of magic, you can start to apply them to your life in a spiritual manner. Remember all acts of magic are aligning with Will, even what appears as your simple desires will lead you, through success and failure, to your higher Will. As you do so, you not only become more aware of your thoughts and emotions and heal injuries of the past, the actions of your higher Will take on significance for your community, country, and the world. As we each fulfill our Will, we continue the Great Work and bring humanity's relationship to a greater perfection with Nature and the Divine.

### Building an Altar

Start by building an altar, a place to remind you of your sacred space. Though we never see Merlin's altar, for it could be said to be all of nature, or in one of his various enclosures, his glass towers or hidden caves with the Thirteen Treasures of Britain, we do find altar building a common practice for magicians all across the globe. An altar can be a simple flat surface dedicated to working with the forces of Nature and the heavens. I would suggest symbols for the four elements – a stone for earth, a red candle for fire, a feather (or incense) for air, and a cup (or bowl) for water. Various traditions arrange the altar in different ways, but as long as you have the four elements and put each in a direction, you will be doing well. My own tradition prefers to have the altar face the north, with the earth object in the north, the fire object in the east, the air object in the south, and the water object in the west. In the center you can place any item that feels right to you, anything symbolic of divinity and your relationship with it. Some put a statue or icon. Others use a plant, crystal, or white candle.

## Meditative State

Get into a more receptive, meditative state beyond the cares of everyday life, to enter your magical awareness. While sitting or standing before your altar, relax your body, starting at the top of your head. Give your head and neck permission to relax. Continue downward through the shoulders, arms, chest, and back. Keep going with the waist, hips, torso, legs, and feet. Count down from twelve to one. You are now in a meditative state ready to do magic. It won't feel all that different. Magical life is not that different from everyday life. The main difference is taking the time to be aware, perceive, and let thought, emotion, and energy flow in a conscious manner.

## Ritual Space and Time

Imagine around you a perfect ring of light. Many traditions suggest it be blue light, as bright blue light is associated with life force, but you can imagine your ring of light in any color you want. Once you feel the ring is around you and your altar, it might fade from your awareness, but have no fear that it is still there. Honor the four directions, one by one in a sun-wise manner. Hold the item of the element up for a moment as you face the direction. I start in the north and move east, south, west, and back to north. Say a personal prayer to divinity, however you perceive the divine, to be with you and guide you. Christian magicians can call upon Jesus, God, Mary, and the angels or saints. Buddhist magicians might call upon the Buddha or the various entities of esoteric Buddhism. Pagans call upon God and Goddess, or even Merlin for help.

## Spell

Once you are in your sacred space, you can perform your specific act of magic, a spell. A spell is simply "spelling out", literally and figurative, what you want in your divine communication. A simple spell to start with is a candle spell. Think of your intention, your desire. What do you wish to create in your life? What color from the chart above suits it? Take a candle of that color. You can write your intention in a few simple words and place the paper under the candle holder. Hold the candle in your circle, and think about your intention. Speak your intention clearly and succinctly. Imagine yourself with the successful results of your intention when you close your eyes. Then open your eyes, and light the candle. Make sure it's secure in the candle holder. Let it burn as long as you can. If it doesn't burn all the way down, snuff it with a candle snuffer or spoon. Don't blow it out. Blowing it out is said to imbalance the perfect energies you've set while snuffing keeps them sealed in and balanced, until you relight it. Continue to relight it and snuff when necessary until the candle is gone. Then the spell is complete and can manifest.

## Release

When your spell is complete, first thank the divine in whatever form you've called upon it. Then thank and release the elements, moving anti-sun-wise from where you started. I would start in the north, then the west, south, and east, and turn again to face the north. Thankfulness to the ever-abundant forces already with you can open you up to more blessings, and help you recognize the blessings you already have. Then imagine your circle dissolving away. If you imagined creating sun-wise, then imagine dissolving it anti-sun-wise. Take a few minutes to sit down and gather your thoughts and energy. Many magicians "ground" excess energy by placing their hands upon the floor and willing the excess energy into the Earth, with the intention of healing the planet, a final act of magic for the ritual.

An example of a simple candle spell a friend did when she believed she was not a magical person was a green candle spell for money. She was trying to sell her house, and even in a good market with no major defects, her house was on the market for over nine months. She tried all sorts of positive thinking and affirmation, but it was the day after she light a green candle in a sacred space, with a paper including her reasonable ideal price, did she get an offer. They closed within thirty days and she believed in the power of magic after that, and eventually went on to study the deeper spiritual aspects of magic.

While the candle spell is a simple form of magic for a specific purpose, another technique is to create magical charms – talismans and amulets are objects imbued with an overall intention such as protection or healing. You can repeat the ritual above, but rather than using a candle spell, take a piece of jewelry you like. Prior to the ritual, place the jewelry under the flow of cold tap water from your faucet to "clear" it of unwanted energies. In the ritual, hold the cleared jewelry and think about your intention. If possible, match the metal to the intention with the previous chart. Gold is a simple and powerful metal for intentions of health, success, and happiness. Silver increases intuition and magical spirituality. Think or speak the words of your intention while holding the jewelry. Envision yourself with those qualities. Fill the charm with your magic, and you have created a powerful talisman. Release the ritual space.

While candles and charms might seem simple and not particularly spiritual at first glance, they are some of the first steps towards deeper magic. When we look at Merlin, legend tells us he was responsible for many magical workings, including shapeshifting, illusions, flight, moving stones across country, and creating invisible towers literally out of thin air. We can't necessarily expect such mythic results, but each of those feats has at its heart a real magical power and ability we can develop with time and practice.

Shapeshifting is a shamanic technique to become more like an animal spirit to learn its lessons. Flight is the gift of soul travel or astral journey. Illusion casting is part of thought projection, and the invisible tower is the creation of the inner temple, the soul shrine. The legend of the stones of Stonehenge can either refer to the ancient technology of the stone age people to build such monuments, the secrets of the past and the knowledge of sacred geometry, or the power of mind over matter, telekinesis, on a massive scale.

## Divination

One can consider magic and spells as a form of speaking to the powers of the universe. If you really seek to have a relationship with the divine, you must also learn to listen. Prayer and meditation are a part of the magical path, but another art often forgotten is traditional in magical societies—divination.

Divination is an act of communing with the divine, usually through established techniques or symbol systems. We can divide divination into

*Buddha, Christ, Merlin*

three major forms. The first is more fluid and psychic. It often requires great skill or training. This is the divination of the psychics and seers, of the prophets and visionaries. Merlin was such a figure, and while we often relate to him primarily as a magician, the oldest texts referring to him more often emphasize his prophetic abilities. Here are some from *The Prophecies of Merlin.* Teacher and author R. J. Stewart believes these prophecies refer to the rise of Hitler, the death of a girl in the waters of the Roman Baths, and the potential for cataclysmic weather in the future.

*"There shall succeed the ass of wickedness, swift against the goldsmiths; but slow against the ravenousness of wolves."*

*"The baths of Badon shall grow cold and their salubrious waters engender death."*

*"The tail of Scorpio shall produce lightning and Cancer quarrel with the Sun. Virgo shall mount upon the back of Sagittarius and darken her virgin flowers. The chariot of the Moon shall disorder the zodiac and the Pleiades break forth into weeping. No offices of Janus shall hereafter return, but his gate being shut shall lie hid in the chinks of Ariadne. The seas shall rise up in the twinkling of an eye and the dust of the ancients shall be restored. The winds shall fight together with a dreadful blast and their sound shall reach the stars."*

Other forms of psychic divination include gazing into a crystal ball, fire, or smoke. This act of gazing is known as scrying. One can see images in the substance and those images will creatively answer a question or predict the future. Similar creative forms of divination can occur through watching the action of melted wax cool in water, or more famously through the leaves on the bottom of a tea cup.

Merlin was a prophet, and while his mysterious and poetic prophecies can be compared to mysterious texts of prophecies from all the major religions, not all of us can easily prophecize. To help compensate, mystics have created what are now known as divination tools or oracle devices. Such tools include tarot cards, as well as rune stones from the Norse and I-Ching symbols from China. Even a simple coin toss, with only two meanings, yes and no, can be considered a divination tool. The symbols in these tools are established, and while some creativity and intuition comes into play, they can be remarkably accurate even if you have no intuitive ability and simply read their meaning from a book. They work through the principle of synchronicity. Synchronicity is a term coined by a modern magician of psychology, C.G. Jung. Essentially, it is the connection between two seemingly unconnected events. The pulling of a Tarot card should have no bearing upon what happens in your future. But to the magician, everything is connected, and one can see the patterns in a system correspond to the reality of life. While magic uses these correspondences in spells to make things happen and create change, divination observes these correspondence to predict the most likely course of events and understand the patterns of the past and present to deal with the future.

While whole books are devoted to the systems of Tarot, Runes, and I-Ching, one can learn quite a bit from simply picking out a divination system and begin using it. Most come with short instructional manuals or booklets that provide a start to deeper study. Obtain one and daily, pull one symbol from it, asking about your day. If you fear self-fulfilling prophecy is at work, rather than true divination, don't look at it until the end of the night, and see how much your chosen symbol corresponds to your day. While this does require a little creative and symbolic thinking and perspective, that is exactly the appropriate mindset to be a successful magician. More complex divinations require several symbols to be pulled or cast, and arranged in specific patterns with meaning. Many believe before you ever do a spell, you should perform a divination, and ask if you "should" perform the spell before you actually do it. I suggest if you seek a magical spirituality, obtain an oracle device such as the tarot, and explore it. You might be surprised at the guidance you receive.

*Buddha, Christ, Merlin*

*Figure 8: The Magician Card from the Tarot*

The last technique is a bridge between the more psychic forms of scrying divination and formal divination systems such as the tarot. It is the experience of omens. Omens are signs from nature and the world around you. Omens can be formally asked for, such as "give me a sign" or come up repeatedly in themes, often three to four times, to get your attention. It is a method by which the universe (or perhaps the intelligence of nature) tries to communicate with you. Encounters with animals, particularly plants or trees and unusual weather phenomenon can occur. In magical societies, every animal, plant, tree, and act of nature has mythology around it, and each myth has a teaching. Likewise, people and (in the modern era) technology can speak to us. Asking a question in prayer or meditation and not receiving a direct answer is quite common, but when someone you encounter, unbidden and unknowingly answers your question for you, the universe is speaking to you. Often the nature of omens is very impersonal to those delivering the messages. Like the animals in the forest, they are unconcerned with our lives in general and don't realize they are giving us the message. The more personal the interaction, the less likely it is an omen from the divine, but it doesn't mean the exchange is not helpful on some level.

Watch for omens and signs in your own life, and ask for them when you need reassurance or guidance as to the direction you are going.

## Immanence in Divinity

One of the key points in making a magical worldview work is the concept that there is no separation between us and the divine. Today we call this immanent divinity, though it was naturally understood before schools of theology arose. While many religions have magical traditions, often labeled "miracles" or "answered prayers" to make them more acceptable theologically, the concept of immanent divinity, the divine in nature, is a major part of Pagan magic. Merlin did arise from a Celtic Pagan worldview, inheriting the spiritual mantle of the Druids. The communication at the core of magic is the communication the magician has with nature and "super nature," the *Anima Mundi,* or soul of the world, another name for Mother Nature or Mother Earth, and the unseen and invisible creator, God or the Great Spirit. Pagan traditions look at each manifestation of nature as having its own intelligence, its own spirit or divinity. Arising out of these traditions comes goddesses of the Moon and gods of the sea, gods of grain and goddesses of rivers and wells, and even deities of abstract human concepts like wisdom, justice, and war.

Modern practitioners relate magical communication to ideas found in science. Many Pagans reference James Lovelock's Gaia Hypothesis. Though using it in ways that he did not necessarily intend, they contend we are all like living organs and cells in the biosphere of the planet, and that the biosphere is alive, calling it Gaia, after the Greek Earth goddess. Each forest is like a lung to the planet. Each river a vein. Humanity, too, is an organ within the body of the Earth, though perhaps we don't quite yet understand our function, or have forgotten it. Just as all the parts of our body work as one, and communicate their needs to each other, we too have that ability with the planet.

Others look to Quantum physics, which postulates the observer and the observed are connected, and the act of observation can affect the outcome. It's not a far stretch to then push for the idea that the intention, the will of the observer can affect the outcome and in essence, perform magic.

Nature-based people understand we are connected, and look to see how their actions will affect future generations and "all their relations" among the animal, plant, and stone people. The web of connection between humanity and the land was depicted in Merlin's time as dragons. The white and red dragons are both allegories for the Saxons and Welsh, but also the intelligence of the land in relation with that nation's collective folk soul. The lands are connected through "dragon lines" also known today as ley lines or faery tracks, said to link the sacred sites of the ancient world. Each is a vortex of spiritual energy where consciousness, nature, and humanity intersect. That is why they were used for ritual, and neolithic sites either took advantage of this fact, or used geomantic magic to connect the lines through the building of the structures.

Many nature-based magical religions are animistic, believing there is an animating, intelligence or spirit, in all things and that you can communicate with it. This is another secret of magic. Everything is alive within the greater body of the divine and can be spoken with, communed with, and its secrets will be revealed. While it might sound far-fetched to many of us today, such insight is the secret of many of our great thinkers, including inventor George Washington Carver. He claimed many of his innovations, particularly around the use of the peanut, came from listening to nature.

Our first attunement with such forces comes from not just observing, but participating in the cycles of the land, Sun, Moon, and stars. Most Pagan and tribal traditions observe the shift of the equinoxes and solstices, the lunar year and agricultural shifts at some point in their development, though different eras of history mark different emphases on solar or lunar reverence.

From attunement with nature and the intelligences of nature, we develop our intuitive powers and can then learn to speak to the plants, trees, and stones as our kin. While they might not always speak back in ways we clearly understand, in time, they reveal their secrets to us. Most in the west think the development of herbalism comes from the scientific trial and error, but most living tribal people today will tell you their herbal knowledge came from the plants themselves, or the voices of the forest and Earth.

## Speaking to Nature

Find a place in nature that calls to you, that feels right for you now. Pay particular attention to trees, rocks, and bodies of water. They are places of power and can embody wise and powerful nature spirits. Get yourself into a meditative state by relaxing your body and counting backwards sitting somewhere in nature. Breathe deeply for a while, breathing in the vital life force of the area, attuning yourself to its spirit. The latin word spiritus means breath, showing how our breath and spirit are connected. When you feel relaxed, ask with an open heart to speak to the spirit of the place, or specifically to the spirit of an individual tree, stone, or body of water there. Listen with an open heart and go with your first impressions. The spirits of nature might "speak" to you in words within your mind, or with images, feelings, or sensations. At first the spirits of nature might be suspicious, as most people have forgotten to do this. Or they might be overjoyed that someone is communing with them. When the dialogue opens up freely, you might get a lot of information at once and have to ask the spirits to slow down, to let you process and understand. You can always ask them to speak to you in a way you clearly understand. Commune with nature for as long as you can. You might want to have a notebook nearby to write down important points for future reflection. Each tree, stone, and river has its own story to tell, its own wisdom to share. Learn to listen and you will understand a key component to spiritual evolution in the magical traditions and be

*Buddha, Christ, Merlin*

well on your way to aligning your will with the divine will found in nature.

## The Wheel of the Year

One of the most powerful ways that those involved in a magical spirituality based in nature can truly commune with nature is to follow the cycles and seasons as expressed in the growing cycles of the Earth. Modern day Pagan magicians follow the Wheel of the Year, an eight spoked festival calendar. While the ancients mostly likely never celebrated it in this current form, the pattern of eight holidays honors many indigenous customs from Europe and across the world. The Wheel of the Year is really an amalgam of the solar holidays, the equinoxes, and the solstices marking particularly alignments of the Sun with the Earth, with the agricultural holidays, also known as "fire festivals."

While indigenous people all around the world have celebrated the solar holidays, in Europe they were particularly marked by the Teutonic people. Living in northern climates, the changes in the Sun's course were particularly important to them. The equinoxes marked days of equal light and dark, while the summer solstice was the time of longest daylight and the winter solstice was the time of longest night, or shortest daylight. The fire festivals are celebrated primarily by the Celtic people, those most strongly associated today with the mysteries of Merlin. They marked the times between the solar holidays and were mostly associated with the cycles of plants and animals.

Together, these eight holidays create a complex and whole pattern to be celebrated by modern Pagans and those seeking to attune to the living spirit of nature. Together, they tell a story of the life of the land as expressed through a primal Goddess and God, each taking fluid and changing roles in nature. The story of their life, love, death, and resurrection can be seen in the seasonal changes, and many of the particular customs found in many modern and Christian holidays, start to make sense when we realize these customs were adopted into the Christian holiday calendar in an effort to get the Pagans to convert over to Christianity. Parallels between the story of the Goddess and God, in a wide variety of forms, and the story of Jesus, are quite intriguing, leading many Pagans to conclude that Jesus was another expression of the seasonal god of the year.

**Yule – Winter Solstice –** Traditionally seen in many pagan cultures as the birth of the God as the sun child. While it is the longest night, the daylight begins to grow as the God of Light grows older and stronger. Traditions of Yule logs, decorating evergreen trees and mistletoe come from the Pagan celebrations of this season.

**Imbolc – Feb 2 –** Imbolc refers to the lactation and milk of the herd sheltered for the winter, ready to give birth to new life. It is considered a fire festival sacred to the Celtic Goddess Brid or Bridget. She is the goddess of poetry, smith-craft and healing, and was later changed into St. Bridget. Candles and light are a big part of this celebration, signaling the awakening of the Earth Goddess, and its modern name is Candlemas.

**Ostara – Spring Equinox –** The day and night are equal but the light is growing and with it rises the Goddess from her rest in the darkness and her winter slumber. As she rises, the land is resurrected with new flowers, budding trees, and the promise of fertility (symbolized by rabbits and eggs). Many of the traditional Easter associations of this time of year are originally from the Teutonic goddess Eostre.

**Beltane – May 1 –** Also known as May Day, it is celebrated with the May Pole dance of intertwining ribbons. The May Pole erection and dance is suggestive of sexual symbolism, uniting the God in the Sky and the Goddess of the Earth through the pole, as the God fathers his future self. The two are young lovers. He is often portrayed at this time as a Green Man. Traditionally it was also celebrated by driving cattle and livestock through two sacred fires to purify them.

**Litha – Summer Solstice –** Known as Midsummer's Eve, the time of twilight is longest on this strange day where they say the realm of humanity overlaps with the realm of the Faery Queen and King. The Sun King is at the peak of his power, but his shadow is the longest, and rises up to battle him. The shadow wins and the light is defeated by darkness.

*Buddha, Christ, Merlin*

The Goddess of the Earth is at the peak of her own power, yet the King and Queen of the land are separated.

**Lammas – The First Harvest.** The God of Light is also seen as the God of Grain, John Barleycorn, and at this time, as the first grains are cut, he is sacrificed and his spirit sent into the darkness of the otherworld. In the Irish tradition, this holiday is known as *Lughnassadh*, the "Funeral Games of Lugh" celebrated with games and parties, and the same happens on this harvest. The dark side of the God rules, but the darkness is not yet obvious. Rituals of grain, beer, and bread are popular.

**Mabon – The Second Harvest.** The God of Light is descending into the underworld, taking the life force with him. The world around him begins to wither and the Goddess of the Earth begins her mourning. The fruits are harvested. Apples in particular are used in ritual. Mabon is the name of a Celtic god of light, a child, lost to the darkness, who is later found by King Arthur.

**Samhain – The Third Harvest.** The animals are slaughtered and the meat salted or smoked to preserve it. The veil between the physical world and the world of the dead is thin. It is an excellent time for divination, as psychic abilities are strong and the spirits wish to speak through our oracles. The dark aspect of the Goddess as crone is said to rule. The dark God walks the land as the master of the hunt, gathering up lost souls to take them to the underworld for rest and regeneration.

While many celebrate the Wheel of the Year in Temple spaces, indoors, it is best whenever possible to get outside at these critical times of shifting energies, and to attune yourself, your body, and your consciousness to the new and shifting consciousness of the Earth, as expressed by the Goddess and God, the divine feminine and masculine. As you continue exploring the magical path, you might find specific cultural traditions that celebrate many of these holidays to your liking and add their traditions to your own, or join their communities.

## Stewardship

A growing understanding in the modern magical and Pagan communities is the concept of stewardship and "green religion." Green religion is when true environmentalism has to take a central focus in the tradition, as the practitioners, whether they identify as Magician, Druid, Witch, Pagan, or by any other label, also identify as steward and caretaker for the Earth and all creatures. If we see the physical as an expression of the divine, rather than a commodity or gift, we are not only responsible, but such actions become an act of worship and veneration in and of itself.

In our modern world of luxuries, environmentalism can seem a daunting and seemingly impossible task. Some magical practitioners go immediately to extremes, making radical lifestyle changes and demanding others do the same, while other start small. We can start by controlling our own day-to-day actions. Choose actions of sustainability. Reduce your own footprint upon the Earth. Reuse and recycle. Educate yourself on the resources in your community, advocate for the policies needed to create more resources, and educate your neighbors on them.

As you live, see the divine in all things, and act accordingly.


While the pagan path is different, parts of it are not so different from the mystical sides of Buddhism and Christianity. The esoteric side of Buddhism, particularly Tibetan Buddhism, has many sorcerous teachings from the indigenous people of Tibet who practiced something we would find similar to shamanism and Witchcraft. Early Christians had a magical cosmology and traces of it are still found in Catholic prayers to the Saints, candle lighting, holy relics, sacred medallions, and teachings on the angels.

Many people believe both Buddha and Christ were master magicians. The difference between them and Merlin, or any other self-identified magician, was the focus. The magician is focused on the manifestation of Divine Will, while the Christian is focused on expressing Divine Love, and the Buddhist on Divine Wisdom. Many of the techniques and ideas grow from the same roots; again showing us there is a perennial wisdom of a greater timeless tradition that can embody all three of these paths.

# Chapter Ten:
# Uniting the Three Ways in Our Age

The three ways are not separate and distinct paths, never touching one another. They are more like the cords of a braid, three threads that are stronger when woven together, and weaker when separate. In religious fervor, adherents of a particular religion look to their own faith as having all the answers, but as they progress on the path of the mystic, they must realize their tradition has paradoxically both all of the answers, and none of them. A depth of understanding can be gleaned by looking at the same questions of life, the same spiritual principles of human existence, from different perspectives.

The occultists of the turn of the twentieth century were well-versed in holding the perspectives of several different traditions at once, and used that to impel them further on the spiritual journey. Each tradition acts like the leg of a stool, providing a stability and support. Dion Fortune is famous for braiding together the mysticism of Christianity with the native land-based Pagan traditions of Britain, and the teaching of Ceremonial Qabala in her life's work.

I myself have found greater understanding from taking a year to study the traditional Hindu text known as *The Baghava Gita* with a teacher who not only explained the history and theology, but asked us to put it into practice through selfless service. Her goal as teacher was not to convert us to Hinduism, but to bring us a deeper experience of our own religion. The class was filled with Christians, a few Jews, a Sikh, three Pagans, and an agnostic. None of us changed faiths, but appreciated the depth of our own path more through understanding the sacred battle found in *The Gita*.

Looking at the timeless truths, even from a perspective that seems alien at first, helps us understand our own perspective and experiences. When approached without the need to defend or justify, but in mutual respect, we realize all paths lead to the same destination, but there is different scenery on each path to appreciate.

Rather than going straight up the spiritual mountain to the top, some spiral upward, spending a little time on many paths, but to have it truly serve us, we have to have a respect and a depth of understanding the paths we travel. Buddhism, Christianity, and Paganism are three fundamental traditions that have served the human experience and are fairly accessible to the modern person. In fact, each of the three areas exemplified in each religion is critical to the evolution of humanity as we progress forward. We need all wisdom teachings and opportunities to look at our own path from different perspectives.

Buddhism is known for its compassion, even though in our discussion, it is the path of Wisdom and the true perception of reality. But in that wisdom, there is a place not for sentimental love, but for true divine love. And for Buddha to persevere in his quest, from spoiled prince to beggar and monk, leading to his liberation under the Bodhi tree, he had to have the will to succeed in his quest, and that personal fortitude led to his Divine Will, even though he left behind the ritual trappings of the esoteric monks and Brahmins. In essence, his life became his magic ritual, his Great Work.

Jesus held great Will. Only someone with such a sense of divine purpose could have had such a difficult ministry. If we look at his crucifixion as a literal truth, for someone to undergo such a horrendous death and remain in a state of grace is nothing short of a complete union of personal will with divine will. While we think of Jesus as passive and peaceful, he expressed strong passion in throwing the money lenders from the Temple. Divine will is the source of his miracles, his own magic. Jesus is also a figure of great wisdom, teaching his message of love with simple parables, images everyone could understand. He found the right approach to reach people, and built upon the wisdom of his people, in the Jewish texts, but reinterpreted them in ways applicable to not only the people of his time, but also to the greater world. He cut through the cultural orthodoxy to the core truth of the teachings.

Merlin the magician embodies will, the divine will of the righteous order of Camelot and, in older teachings, the Goddess of the land herself. He moves mysteriously from place to place, but always with purpose.

Yet the wizard archetype is known for embodying wisdom. Wizards and Witches are known as the wise ones, the cunning folk who know the secrets hidden by nature. This wisdom is the source of their magic. While we rarely think of Merlin, or Paganism in general as a tradition of love, Merlin is seemingly undone by his love for his apprentice Nimue. Paganism today, particularly in the revival of Wicca, embodies the principles of Perfect Love and Perfect Trust, the unconditional love found in all wisdom traditions. Our love is the love found in nature.

The three principles are found in all religions, delving beyond dogma and social conditioning, into the realm of personal experience and mysticism. You cannot walk the path of the mystic without finding these eternal truths in some form. They are found in the struggle of reconciling our human nature with our super human nature, our divine nature. All these traditions recognize the inherently human and inherently divine sides of their wise founders. This dual nature is a fundamental truth to the mystic. Reconciliation is the secret of the ages, the heart of the ancient mystery schools, and the culmination of the Great Work of the philosophers.

Jesus is touted by his followers as the "son of God." His divine parentage is emphasized the most, and sometimes used to divide us from his life experience. Many interpret this "son of God" teaching as we are all children of God, and we realize it when we awaken to our divine, Christ-like nature, as Jesus did in his life. He was also very mortal, with doubts, fears, angers, and love.

While not emphasized as much, Siddhartha , born in the lap of luxury, was marked in many ways as divine, the potential Buddha, through physical traits. He too was visited by sages, wise men to confirm his divine nature. But he still struggled for liberation, finding his own way, as many of us do.

In esoteric tradition, Merlin is technically referred to as a *cambion*, part human and part otherworldly, and very powerful. Either seen as a child of the gods and faeries, or fathered by the Devil or a demon, he is otherworldly, and his story is reconciling those two natures, human and otherworldly, or good and evil. That is the story of Camelot in many ways: the ideal set by Nature and embodied by chivalry and the failings of humanity, to live up to that ideal.

When we awaken to the religion beyond dogma or orthodoxy, the underlying perennial wisdom, we awaken to the dual nature that is a part of all of us. Prior to this awakening, or perhaps just after its realization, we wander in the wilderness. While many wander in life, as if in some sort of daydream, others purposely wander in the wilderness, the Wasteland. Buddha leaves the comfort of his home and suffers, often by choice, in the material world beyond his castle's walls. Merlin wanders the forest, driven mad by the savageries of warfare and bloodshed. Jesus wanders the desert, tempted by Satan to renounce his coming ministry for dominion over the world. Each of these wise men reconciles the extremes of the world, and thereby their own nature and then embraces their calling to serve the world.

Some traditions make the mistake of emphasizing one aspect of our dual nature over the other. Renounce the material world and embrace solely the spiritual. Renounce the spiritual as unknown and unknowable and enjoy the world. The key is the paradox. Both are right. Neither is right.

We have to create the conditions within our consciousness where we can hold both our human and divine natures simultaneously, and live from both simultaneously. Both are necessary in this life. Neither is better than the other. Our mystical traditions, meditation practices, rituals, and philosophies challenge us. They shape our consciousness into an appropriate vessel to embrace this paradox and live a remarkable life with the world, immersed in spirit, not separate. I believe all great spiritual leaders and teachers have passed through this point of paradox, even if they did not recognize it as such.

The foundation, the tripod to solidly hold our newly developed container of consciousness, is forged from Wisdom, Love, and Will. All three are needed to hold us upright, even though we might face and see only one point. The other two await us in the shadows, informing our experience indirectly, if not directly.

The three ways are also illustrated through the relationship our three wise men have with the three worlds. Cultures across the world look at the spirit world as divided into three realms, characterized as an overworld, underworld, and middle world. Most are familiar with them as heaven, hell, and earth, though the Christianized vision of heaven and hell is not the only way to perceive these realms. The overworld is seen as a realm of eternal perfection and an overall perspective. The realm of the earth is the place of time and space, of process and change. The underworld is a place of challenge and change, power and blessing. It is a place of rest, regeneration, and challenge.

These three worlds are most often described in the traditions of shamanism. A shaman is a term for the healer of a tribal culture, who specifically heals by mediating between the tribe of humanity and the worlds of spirit. The word shaman has been translated variously as fire, song, or secret, meaning the shaman is a mediator who has hidden knowledge. While traditionally a shaman refers to such a healer in Siberia, and has expanded to Asia, and even to refer to practitioners in Native American traditions, the term has been expanded to a series of techniques and a worldview. Each of these wise men could be considered a shaman in the broadest sense of the word, and their relationship with the three worlds gives us a certain amount of insight to their own spiritual missions.

The three worlds are connected by a spire, an axis. Mythology is filled with such images, ranging from Mount Olympus to Jacob's Ladder, but the most common image is the tree. The heavens are held up by its branches. The trunk is the axis around which the world turns. The roots dig deep into the underworld. Each of our wise men has a relationship with a special tree.

Buddha begins his journey like us, in the Middle World. He comes to the world tree as the Bodhi Tree. While there, he is tormented by underworld forces, a demon, even though he never leaves the tree. Eventually he awakens to the perfection of the heavens and attains his Buddha-hood. The tree then became the place where he reached enlightenment, and for us, becomes both a symbol and a path to do the same. Buddha brings the wisdom of the heavens to the earth. His wisdom tradition seeks to bring perfection and detachment of the heavens to the world of humanity, to give freedom from the suffering found in the world of space and time.

Jesus also begins his journey in the Middle World, though he is more touched by the heavens. Said to be the son of God, his birth was announced by angels – heavenly creatures. But he is born of woman in the world and his teaching of love focuses on the love of the heavens from the Heavenly Father. In his forty days in the desert, Jesus comes face to face with the forces of Satan, the tradition's perception of the ruler of the underworld. His axis mundi, his world tree, is the cross of the crucifixion. Rather than sitting at its base in the middle world, he is elevated by the cross towards the heavens. Through his sacrifice and suffering, he is focused on heaven and his ascension. His teachings focused on the rise out of this world, the promise of salvation, and the perfection of another realm, above and beyond. It is said he harrowed the depths of hell from the time between his death and his resurrection and eventual ascension.

Merlin's whole life is about trees, the forest, and the wild. Yet he has a special relationship with one tree. While some of the myths depict him trapped in a tower, crypt, or crystal cave by his lovely Nimue, another less well-known image is being trapped in the Hawthorne tree. Hawthorne has been associated with Christ as well, being a thorn tree, like the crown worn by Christ on the cross. Merlin's imprisonment is in the tree, either the trunk of the middle world, or in a cavern beneath its roots, the cave of the underworld held tight by the tree. While he is a starry prophet, he interprets the light of the heavens down into the world of men with his prophetic visions and verse. He draws down the starlight as the tree's leaves draw down the sunlight. He wanders the woods of the Middle World, but eventually his resting place is in the great below of the underworld, the place of rest and regeneration. For those of us who still hear his call to magic and nature, we know the true source of nature comes from below, as things issue forth from the Earth in her greenery. He mediates the magic and wisdom of the depths to the world of space and time.

Each of our wise men's traditions has a different focus and it can be helpful to compare the three to understand them better, and see a world view that includes all three realms.

| BUDDHISM | CHRISTIANITY | PAGANISM |
| --- | --- | --- |
| No personal god | Personal god | Many gods, both personal and impersonal forces of nature from one source |
| Buddha is not considered to be divine | Jesus Christ is the divine son of God | Everyone is divine, for the world is an expression of divinity |
| Our future is determined by the karma of our past and present | Sins are forgiven through Christ | Karma or Wyrd is simply the result of our actions, change your fate |
| Enlightenment is found by your own work and effort | Salvation is attained through a belief in Christ | Enlightenment is attained through action in the world. One must do their "Great Work" in the world. |
| Meditate to reach enlightenment | Pray for salvation | Perform magic to become one with divinity |

While there are timeless similarities between the three wisdom traditions depicted here, there are also some fundamental differences. The differences don't necessarily illustrate the wrongness of any one tradition. That kind of polarity thinking of absolute right and wrong is dissolving away as we look at the wisdom of three, where there is a connecting force between extremes. Each religion, from those presented here, to the many other world faiths not mentioned in detail, have a perspective on the truth. One perspective is not absolute for humanity's understanding, even from what might appear to be an enlightened teacher, guru, messiah, or buddha. Taoists have a saying, from Lao Tsu's *Tao Te Ching*, the Tao, meaning the Way, that can be named is not the eternal Tao. Though the Taoists have their own particular slant on reality, I think this bit of Taoist advice is a good guide for us all.

Being rooted in a tradition helps us grow and develop in reference to that tradition. It gives us a proven path and framework, but can only take us so far. You can believe your tradition has the hold on absolute truth. In my journey among mystics, I've noticed the more direct experiences you have, the less dogmatic you are about your truth. You recognize the wisdom of those who had similar understandings and experiences, even in completely different religious contexts. There isn't a need to argue, fight, or convince the other about the correctness of your own path. Each is free to pursue the truth as they see it, with the knowledge we are all heading in the same direction eventually.

In our global culture, the wisdom of the East is best exemplified in the form of Buddhism. In many ways, Buddhism took some of the key concepts of Hinduism, with a bit of a different interpretation, and put it in a form that could be exported beyond the bounds of India. Although Hindu religious practices can be adopted by those outside of India or Indian descent, much of the practice is tied directly to the culture, history, languages, and land of India. Buddhism kept basic tenets of Eastern perspective and was able to expand throughout Asia, with each culture absorbing it and adapting it to their own traditions, yet retaining the basic core of Buddhism. From the East it has spread worldwide, along with teachings of Hinduism and Taoism, bringing important Eastern concepts to the Western world and awakening the West's own search for spiritual expression.

The wisdom of the West has been distilled into Christianity. Christianity took the texts of Judaism, a mainly tribal religion based upon culture and birth, and gave it wider context and meaning. For

*Buddha, Christ, Merlin*

Christians, the life of Jesus became the fulfillment of the Old Testament prophecies. Unlike Islam, there is an appeal to the message of Jesus to the general western psyche and westerners have been able to accept it even when there is a cognitive dissonance between the message of Christ and the actions of the Church. Unlike the Buddhist expressions that more readily expressed the cultural context of native traditions, Christianity only adopted the elements of native Pagan beliefs when necessary to retain converts, such as the seasonal holidays, and actively encouraged the dismissal of the deeper teachings, vilifying the practices of adherents of Paganism as devil worship and malicious magic. We now live in an era where the folk elements of Christian tradition are mostly forgotten. Who knows that much about the origin of All Saints Day or Candlemas? Who knows how eggs and bunnies got wrapped up into Easter, or trees, logs, and mistletoe into Christmas? Not many. Though some Buddhist strains attempted to suppress native wisdom, particularly in Tibet, it was nothing like the systemized and widespread propaganda of the Western Christian Church.

Yet mystics have used the rich symbolism of the Christian tradition for their own practices when working in the Christian era. While some might have used Christianity as a cover, others were most likely faithful Christians, using both mysticism and Christian devotion on their quest for enlightenment. Christianity was adopted into the study of Jewish Kabalah, creating the more Christianized forms of Cabala. Alchemists looked at the resurrection of Christ as the gold of the Philosopher's Stone, turning lead, or sin, into redemption. Many operated wholly in a Christian context and were celebrated as saints, such as St. Francis of Assisi or St. Theresa of Avila. Ceremonial magicians of the late nineteenth and early twentieth centuries brought all of this lore under one banner as the Western Mysteries, just as Theosophists with mostly Eastern material.

At first glance the systems of the East and West appear contradictory, the battle between impersonal and the personal. The connecting force in our triad is the native magical lore found in both the East and West. Similar world views are found among tribal people all around the world.

While by no means an exact match, you see similar mythologies, theologies, and rituals among the "Pagan" people of Europe, but also their counterparts in the Americas, Africa, and Asia. The regeneration of the various Pagan traditions today under the banners of NeoPaganism, Heathenism, Druidry, Wicca, Witchcraft, Asatru, and Faery Faith, point to the growing frustration many feel with their mainstream religious options, and how they seek magic as the bridge between potentially contradictory worldviews. The nature of magic is paradox. Two different things can be held simultaneously without breaking. The nature of magic is to do the impossible, and with it, we can create new and different paradigms where every path has merit.

While most think of magic as speaking to the universe, asking for what you want, magic is actually a combination of prayer and meditation. When we pray, we speak to the divine, either in prescribed ritual or in our own heartfelt words. When we meditate, we first listen to ourselves and eventually listen in still silence for direction from the divine, however we see it. Magic combines prayer and meditation. It's a living communion with the divine, and most magicians have times when they speak to, pray, or make magic with intention, and other times when they are quiet, introspective, and listening for advice before taking action. Magic bridges the divide between those who simply pray and those who simply meditate. It allows a back and forth dialogue, a co-creation between us and the universe. When you learn to look with "eyes that see" as they say in the magical traditions, you find magic in every religious tradition, surviving in places even where it's been repressed. The three wise men of Jesus' nativity were Magi, from a different time and place, but magicians nonetheless, with a wide worldview of the timeless wisdom of all religions.

We are leaving a time of duality and entering into a new consciousness, a new age. Previously everything was above and below, light and dark, good and evil. Now, we are leaving those dualistic ways of looking at either this or that, and looking at the whole. To transition into this new way of thinking, we need transitional concepts, bridges between the extremes, to show how they are connected.

We need to move from a world of two, of duality, to a world of three and plurality while still seeing the greater whole. You cannot have above and below without between, which is really where humanity stands. You cannot have light and dark without the colors of the rainbow. You cannot have good and evil without acknowledging the complexity of emotion and motivation between the two extremes. It is between and around these extremes where you find God. God is in all things.

Part of our transition includes the concept that we are all necessary. The universe has no "spare parts". Each of us has a unique role to fulfill, and we only fulfill it when we are in tune with our essential self. It does not get fulfilled when we live as we believe others wish us to live. It is another paradox. Only when I am my individual self, do I really serve the greater community. By sublimating my sense of self, I actually hurt the overall community, depriving it of me and what I am really meant to do and who I am meant to be.

Three is the transitional concept, moving us from "you verses me" to "us". Three will bring us from a vertical hierarchy of those above and below to a horizontal or circular "hierarchy" where we are equal but different. The three of Will, Love, and Wisdom bridges the gap between religious movements, three different and major branches such as Paganism, Christianity, and Buddhism, but once you understand these three concepts you'll see them in Judaism, Islam, Hinduism, and in lesser known religion such as Ba'hai, Sikhism, and Thelema. Love, Will, and Wisdom help us attune to our authentic selves, for if we embody these three principles we cannot present a false sense of self to the world or to our own consciousness. There is no room for falsehood when you are acting from Love, Will, and Wisdom.

We can help bridge these gaps for ourselves and the world by finding our Wise Women and Wise Men, looking in our own traditions and culture, but also looking for these three key concepts beyond our comfort zones. We can find role models and stories that serve to connect us to those we once thought of as "other" and alien to us. Buddha,

Christ, and Merlin are only the first three; there are many more to explore. We look to those who have answers to the questions we all have about ourselves and our lives. We look to those who successfully answer the big questions of who, what, when, where, and why? Some are religious. Some are mythic, and some are found in activism, politics, education, and right in our own neighborhoods. By finding such figures, we find patterns to emulate and inspire so we too, can be well on our way to becoming Wise Ones who will then go out and inspire. Through Love and Will, grow Wise and fulfill your Great Work in the world.

# Glossary

**Adam Kadmon:** The archetypal pattern for humanity in the Jewish mystical tradition.

**Alchemy:** The tradition of transmutation most famous for seeking to turn lead into gold, but truly transforming the soul into a state of conscious perfection. Alchemy has had expressions in Asia, the Middle East and Europe, in Pagan, Jewish, Christian and Islamic forms, though many claim this spiritual science began in Egypt.

**Aleister Crowley:** Controversial prophet of the religion of Thelema, and notable occult scholar and magician.

**Ambrosius Aurelianus:** The King that followed Vortigern and preceded Arthur's father, Uther.

**Amulet:** A charm that is usually protective in nature, removing unwanted forces.

**Anapanasati:** Mindfulness of Breath. Buddhist breathing meditation practice.

**Anima Mundi:** Alchemical name for Mother Nature, meaning "spirit of the world".

**Arthur Pendragon:** King of Camelot. Son of Uther. Pupil of Merlin. Associated with the totem of the Bear.

**Arthurian Mythos:** The wide range of story, folklore, and mythology associated with King Arthur, Merlin, Camelot, and the Avalon.

**Asatru:** A specific form of Heathenism focusing on the worship of the Aesir, or sky gods of Norse mythology.

**Asita:** a holy man and ascetic who lived in the Himalayan mountains. He tutored Sudhodana and proclaimed Siddhartha would be a great king or holy man.

**Astral Travel:** The ability to project yourself beyond the physical body to see other locations in this world (remote viewing) or other non-physical worlds entirely.

**Astrologer:** One who practices the art and science of astrology, the movement of the heavens, to understand the conditions upon the Earth. The Magi were traditionally associated with astrology and star gazing.

**Asuras:** The lower deities of Buddhism.

**Atlantis:** A mythic land believed to once have existed between America and Europe/Africa. The home of an advanced, but eventually corrupt civilization. The nation eventually sunk under the ocean.

**Aurelius Clemens Prudentius:** Author of the poem *Psychomachia* with the teachings of the Seven Deadly Sins of Christianity.

**Avalon:** Apple Land. The mysterious otherworld of Arthurian Mythos ruled by the Lady of the Lake.

**Bailey, Alice:** A former Theosophist who went on to "channel" a number of extremely influential esoteric books. She is responsible for channeling the pioneering, detailed information on the Seven Rays.

**Bethlehem:** The town where Jesus was born.

**Blavatsky, Helena P.:** The cofounder of Theosophy and the author of *Isis Unveiled* and *The Secret Doctrine*.

**Blue Ray:** The Second Ray, the Ray of Divine Love.

**Bodhisattva:** Buddhist practitioners who achieve individual liberation and attain a state where they use wisdom to aid all sentient beings in liberation. The Bodhisattvas are emphasized on the Mahayana School of Buddhism.

**Bornless One:** The Higher Self, the Soul, in Thelema.

**Brahma:** The creator aspect of divinity in Hinduism.

**Buddha:** The Awakened One. Referring to Prince Siddhartha as the founder of Buddhism but also everyone's own Buddha nature that must be awakened. One of the Three Jewels of Buddhism.

**Cardinal Virtues:** Temperance, Wisdom, Justice and Courage. Their origins are in the writings of Aristotle and Plato.

**Channa:** Siddhartha's charioteer.

**Charm:** An object infused with a magical intention or spell.

**Christ Consciousness:** The consciousness associated with Jesus Christ, specifically the level of spiritual consciousness associated with unconditional love, sacrifice, forgiveness, and harmony. The state of unconditional love that Christ holds and those who seek to be Christian aspire to attain. In Qabalistic lore, it is associated with the center of the Tree of Life, Tiphereth, and the astrological body of the Sun. In Theosophical lore, the Second Ray, or Blue Ray, is associated with Christ Consciousness.

**Crone:** The destructive aspect of the Goddess in Modern Wicca.

**Cycle of Samsara:** The cycle of suffering and rebirth.

**Dalai Lama:** The leader of the Gelugpa school of Tibetan Buddhism and the spiritual and political leader of Tibet, currently in exile. Believed by Tibetan Buddhists to be an incarnation of a Tibetan Bodhisattva. The current Dalai Lama is the fourteenth.

**Dee, John:** A British magician, alchemist, and possible secret agent with the codename 007. Responsible, along with his partner Edward Kelley, for receiving the Enochian Angel system of magic.

**Deosil:** "Sun-wise." Clockwise in the northern hemisphere

**Devas:** The higher deities of Buddhism, often used to reference nature spirits in New Age writings.

**Dharma:** Right action. In Buddhism, following the teachings of the Buddha. One of the Three Jewels of Buddhism.

**Dion Fortune:** A ceremonial magician who is most famous for her occult novels *The Sea Priestess* and *Moon Magic,* and her work on the Qabalah. Dion worked with the system of the Rays as well, mixing Christianity, British Arthurian folklore, and Hermetic Qabalah.

**Divine Will:** The True Will of the creator. We each have an individual Divine Will, known as our True Will.

**Druid:** A Celtic caste of priest-magicians, responsible for guiding Celtic communities, dispensing law, maintaining religious services, and keeping mythic, historic, and genealogical records of the community through oral tradition. Merlin is associated with the Druidic tradition.

**Enoch:** Old Testament figure who ascended into heaven bodily.

**Eucharist:** A sacrament of holy communion involving bread and wine, reenacting the Last Supper. Catholics believe the bread and wine is literally transubstantiated into the body and blood of Christ.

**Excalibur:** King Arthur's second sword, given as a gift by the Lady of the Lake. The scabbard prevents its wearer from bleeding. Not the fabled Sword in the Stone, Arthur's first sword.

**Faery Faith:** A pseudo-Pagan tradition based upon the amalgam of Pagan Faery Teaching and Faery teaching from a post Christianized era, particularly focusing on the British Isles.

**Frankincense:** A resin used as incense in many temple traditions.

**Gabriel:** One of the four more well known of the archangels, along with Michael, Raphael, and Uriel. The angelic messenger who told Mary about her pregnancy with Jesus.

**Gaia:** Also Gaea. The Greek Earth Mother Goddess.

**Gautama:** Family name of Siddhartha that he was known by when a monk.

**Geoffrey of Monmouth:** The author of the *History of the Kings of Britain,* as well as *The Prophecies of Merlin* and *The Life of Merlin.* He is responsible for setting the historic and mythic stage for later work on King Arthur, Merlin, and Camelot.

**Gold:** One of the three gifts brought to Jesus by the Wise Men. In alchemy, gold is equated with enlightenment. An alchemist who creates the Philosopher's Stone can change base metals into gold.

**Great Work:** Latin *Magnum Opus.* The Western concept of enlightenment. Union with the divine through fulfilling your "work" and purpose in the world and in the realm of spirit.

**Gwenievere:** Queen of Camelot and wife to King Arthur.

**Heathenism:** A modern revival of the northern "Pagan" traditions, often divorced from traditional occult themes and cultures.

**Hercules:** A Greek and Roman demigod, fathered by the god Zeus and a human mother Alcmeme. He underwent twelve challenges, symbolic of the twelve Zodiac signs, and ascended to Mount Olympus to live with the gods.

**Hermetics:** A collected body of philosophical and practical teachings attributes to Hermes and mythically associated with the Egyptian god Thoth. Hermeticism has adopted lore from both the East and West, and most often involved ancient Pagan philosophy, alchemy and Qabalah.

**Herod Anitpas:** King of Judea and son of Herod the Great. Reigned at the time of Jesus' crucifixion.

**Higher Self:** The part of us that is wholly divine and all knowing. The Soul.

**Hinduism:** The religious traditions of India.

**Holy Grail:** A sacred relic that can heal and redeem the Wasteland. Pagans see it as a gift from the Goddess taking the shape of a cauldron, chalice, spear, plate, stone, or even severed head. Most Christianized myths associate it with the cup of the Last Supper, though it can take any of those forms.

**Holy Shekinah:** The third aspect of the Catholic Trinity, better known as the Holy Ghost or Holy Spirit, the inherent wisdom manifest in the world.

**Horus:** An Egyptian deity of warfare, light, and fire. Equated with the Son in the Trinity.

**Hybornea:** A mythic paradise nation existing somewhere in the north.

**I-Ching:** A system of divination used in Taoism, consisting of 64 hexagrams, or patterns of lines, each with a unique meaning.

**Incubus:** Described by Christianity as a male demon that seduced women into unholy sexual union. The female version of this demon, seducing men, is known as a Succubus.

**Inner Temple:** A vision of an inner sacred space. Also known as the Soul Shrine.

**Isis:** An Egyptian goddess, wife, and sister of Osiris, and mother to Horus. Equated with the Mother in the Trinity.

**Jacob's Ladder:** A Jewish image of the cosmic axis or world "tree."

**John:** One of the Apostles and considered an author of one of the four recognized Gospels.

**John the Baptist:** A prophet preceding Jesus, who recognized Jesus and baptized him in the river. John was reportedly also a cousin to Jesus.

**Joseph of Arimathea:** A disciple of Jesus who reportedly brought the Holy Grail to England in esoteric Christian tradition.

**Kabalah:** A form of Jewish mysticism, later fused with non-Jewish teachings, using the Tree of Life as a lens to view the world, to form Christian Cabala, and Hermetic Qabalah.

**Kantaka:** Siddhartha's horse.

**Karma:** "Action." The result of your actions, including your intentions, thoughts, and words.

**Kilesa:** Defilements that prevent us from reaching nirvana.

**King Herod:** King of Judea at the time of Jesus' birth. Christian mythos tells us that he ordered the death all male children born at the time to prevent the rise of the Messiah.

**Koan:** A literary teaching tool of a riddle, question, paradox, or fable that is designed to aid a student of Zen Buddhism on the quest of enlightenment.

**Lao Tzu:** The founder of Taoism and a great Chinese sage.

**Last Supper:** The last meal Jesus shared with his apostles before his death, when he taught them the ritual of the Eucharist.

**Lemuria:** A mythic land believed to be somewhere in the Pacific. A technologically primitive but spiritually evolved culture lived there before it eventually sank. Generally believed to predate Atlantis.

**Ley Lines:** Lines of energy surrounding the Earth, like global acupuncture meridians. Also known as Dragon Lines and associated with earthy, serpentine energy.

**Limbini:** The village where Siddhartha was born.

**Luke:** An early Christian considered to be an author of one of the four recognized Gospels.

**Magi:** An ancient Persian priestly caste in the Zoroastrian tradition. The word forms the basis of our term magician.

**Maha Pajapati:** Siddhartha foster mother, sister of Queen Maya.

**Mahacohen:** Literally "much master" or the enlightened master who is the Lord of Civilization, guiding the evolution of humanity.

**Mahayana:** One of the two major schools of Buddhism. Usually translated as "Great Vehicle."

**Maiden:** The generative or creative aspect of the Goddess in modern Wicca.

**Manu:** The archetypal "first" man.

**Mara:** A demon that tempted Gautama, trying to prevent him from attaining Buddha-hood.

**Mark:** An early Christian considered an author of one of the four recognized Gospels.

**Mary:** The mother of Jesus. Also known as Mother Mary or Saint Mary.

**Mary Magdalene:** A disciple of Jesus Christ. Considered a reformed prostitute by traditional Christianity. Mystics often see her as a priestess, partner, and even potential wife to Jesus.

**Matthew:** One of the Apostles and considered an author of one of the four recognized Gospels.

**Maya:** Queen. Wife to Sudhodana and mother to Siddhartha. In Hinduism, the term for the "illusion" of reality.

**Mercury:** In alchemy, the symbol of the fluid connecting principle, as well as the spirit.

**Messiah:** Literally "anointed one." Usually refers to a political or spiritual liberator.

**Mohamed:** The last prophet, according to Islam. Responsible for receiving the Qur'an and founding Islam.

**Morgana Le Fey:** Morgana of the Faeries. Sometimes considered the original Lady of the Lake. Other times she is depicted as Arthur's half-sister, and often a villain in the Arthurian mythos.

**Moses:** A Jewish Old Testament prophet responsible for leading the Jewish people out of Egypt and for receiving the Ten Commandments. Many believe Moses was trained in the courts of Egypt as a magician.

**Mother:** The sustaining aspect of the Goddess in Modern Wicca.

**Mount Olympus:** A Greek mythic image of the cosmic axis or world "tree."

**Myrrh:** A bitter resin used in burial rites and burned as incense.

**Mystic's Will:** Another name for True Will. Also a reference to the occultist's ability to focus beyond that of most ordinary people.

**Naraka:** Hell. A place of suffering.

**NeoPaganism:** The "new" or modern revival of Paganism.

**Nirvana:** The state of supreme liberation as described in the Buddhist traditions.

**Non-self:** The Buddhist concept of the soul, differing from the concept of an individual and eternal soul.

**Om Mani Padme Hum:** "The Jewel in the Lotus." Tibetan Buddhist mantra.

**Omen:** A sign from nature answering a question asked or giving a message for those who have not asked.

**Orpheus:** Greek mythic figure said to have visited Hades while still alive before returning to the living world. Associated with the Orphic Mystery Schools of ancient Greece.

**Osiris:** An Egyptian deity of both agriculture and the underworld. Equated with the Father in the Trinity.

**Paganism:** Drawn from a Latin term referring to country dwellers, the name Pagan eventually meant those who practiced rural religions and did not convert over to Christianity. Pre-Christian European traditions. Modern Paganism is technically NeoPaganism, or new Paganism.

**People of the Book:** Practitioners of the three major prophetic religions originating in the Middle East – Judaism, Christianity, and Islam. All three are noted for the primary importance of scripture as divine communication.

**Preta:** The level of invisible spirits filled with strong desires and pain.

**Principle of Correspondence:** "As Above, So Below." One of the seven Hermetic Principles.

**Quetzalcoatl:** A Mayan savior god associated with light and the plumed serpent. Sometimes compared to Jesus Christ.

**Rahula:** Siddhartha's son.

**Red Ray:** The First Ray, the Ray of Divine Will.

**Reiki:** A lineage based tradition of hands-on and distant healing founded by Dr. Mikao Usui. Based upon Japanese Buddhist traditions, but adopted into a wide variety of metaphysical and alternative health systems.

**Rev. John Henry Hopkins:** Composed the Christmas carol *We Three Kings of Orient Are* in 1857.

**Round Table:** The table around which Arthur and his knights gathered. Symbolic of the wheel of the Zodiac and its twelve constellations.

**Runes:** A Teutonic system of divination and magic consisting of a variety of symbols. The two most popular traditional systems are known as the Elder Futhark and the Younger Futhark.

**Saint:** In the Catholic tradition, figures so virtuous and touched by God that they become conduits for miracles and after death on Earth become vehicles to dispense divine grace. The type of grace they dispense is based upon the life they led or the roles they held. Christian folk magic involves petitioning the saints in particular ways to obtain aid and answered prayers.

**Salt:** In alchemy, the symbol for the fixed and solid principle, as well as the body.

**Sangha:** Buddhist community. One of the Three Jewels of Buddhism.

**Satan:** The Adversary of Christian mythology, equated with Lucifer, the Serpent in the Garden of Eden and the Islamic Shaitan. In esoteric teachings, Satan is an archangel associated with the forces of adversity, acting as an accuser or prosecutor on the behalf of the divine, and is not related to any mythology of fallen angels.

**Shamanism:** Tribal traditions of working directly with the spirits to create healing, change, and protection. The term originates in Siberia, but has come to denote tribal spirit workers in many areas, particularly Asia and the Americas.

**Shambhala:** A mythic city most often cited in or near Tibet that is said to be populated by enlightened masters and a model for the perfect society.

**Shapeshifting:** A technique where a practitioner feels themselves taking on the energy, shape and mannerisms of another animal or object, usually in vision.

**Shinto:** A nature spirit based religion of Japan.

**Shiva:** The destroyer aspect of divinity in Hinduism.

**Siddhartha:** The man who would become Buddha.

**Sophia:** Wisdom. The feminine principle found in mystical Christianity.

**Spell:** A specific act of magic.

**Star of Bethlehem:** The "star" that guided the three Wise men to Jesus.

**Sudhodana:** King and father to the man who would become Buddha.

**Sulfur:** In alchemy, the symbol of the volatile creative principle, as well as the individual soul.

**Talisman:** A charm that is usually manifesting in nature, bringing you a specific blessing or wish.

**Tantra:** Systems of often mystical teachings found in Buddhism and Hinduism.

**Taoism:** A philosophical and religious practice of China. The Tao is known as "the Way" and forms the basis of much of China's esoteric lore.

**Tarot:** A deck of seventy-eight cards divided into 22 Major Arcana and 56 Minor Arcana used for divination and magic. Each card has associations with the elements, planets, and occult symbolism.

**Telekinesis:** The psychic talent to move physical objects with the mind alone. Also known as psychokinesis.

**The Baghava Gita:** A Hindu text focused on Arjuna, a warrior and the god Krishna acting as his charioteer and teacher.

**The Four Noble Truths:** The foundational teaching of Buddhism. 1. Life means suffering. 2. The Origin of Suffering is Attachment. 3. The cessation of Suffering is Possible. 4. The Path leads to the Cessation of Suffering.

**The Noble Eightfold Path:** Eight points of action that will end suffering according to Buddhist teachings.

**Thelema:** Greek for "will." The name of Aleister Crowley's religion for the new aeon, based upon Love, Will, and Magick through his prophetic writing known as *The Book of the Law* or *Liber al vel Legis*.

**Theological Virtues:** Faith, Hope, and Charity, added to the four cardinal virtues with the advent of Christian theology.

**Theosophy:** The study of God Wisdom. A modern spiritual movement co-founded by Helena P. Blavatsky.

**Theravada:** One of the two major branches of Buddhism. Usually translated as "School of the Elders."

**Thirteen Treasures of Britain:** Thirteen sacred relics collected by Merlin and hidden in his enclosure or cave.

**Three Marks of Existence:** Impermanence, suffering, and the non-self.

**Tibetan Buddhism:** A branch of the Mahayana school of Buddhism that fused with, and sometimes came in conflict with, the native folk customs and beliefs of Tibet.

**Trinity:** The three primary forces of the universe, described differently in every religious tradition.

**True Will:** The fulfillment of your soul's purpose in every moment. The western cognate to Dharma.

**Uther Pendragon:** Father to King Arthur. Associated with dragons, creatures linked with the living power of the land.

**Vajrayana:** The "diamond vehicle" of Mahayana Buddhism.

**Vishnu:** The preserver aspect of divinity in Hinduism.

**Viviane:** A name most associated with the Lady of the Lake, along with Morgan and Nimue in various Arthurian stories. Priestess of the feminine mysteries and the enchanted land of Avalon.

**Vortigern:** The King who ostensibly ruled Britain when Merlin was a child.

**Wasteland:** The state of the world after the disharmony between King Arthur and Queen Gwenievere, or after the crimes committed by another king. The condition represents the disconnection and fall from nature and divinity that many people regularly feel when out of harmony with nature and the divine. The quest of the Holy Grail is the quest to heal the Wasteland.

**Watcher:** The Higher Self, the Soul. Also a name for a fallen angel.

**Wheel of the Year:** A modern adaption of the solar and agricultural cycle of holidays, celebrated by Neopagans and Witches.

**Wicca:** One popular expression of modern Witchcraft. It can refer to an eclectic and sometimes solitary practice, or a formal and initiatory lineage based tradition. Sometimes specifically divided into Eclectic Wicca or Modern Wicca, and British Traditional Wicca or simply Traditional Wicca. Sometimes Wicca is used to indicate the religion of Witchcraft, while the "Craft" refers to the spells and no religious teachings.

**Wiccan Rede:** The guiding moral teaching of Wicca, a form of modern Witchcraft. It is summed up with the lines, "And it harm none, do as ye will."

**Widdershins:** "Anti–sunwise." Counterclockwise in the northern hemisphere.

**Witch:** A practitioner of the often misunderstood wisdom tradition of Witchcraft. The popular modern revival of Witchcraft is often known today as Wicca, though there are many Witches who do not identify with the term Wiccan.

**Witchcraft:** A specific form of NeoPaganism where the practitioners identify as Witches, drawing inspiration from priestesses and priests of ancient Pagan traditions, all the way to the village Witch and cunning man. Witches perform rituals, spells, and usually follow a magical spiritual path. Not all Witches identify with the term Wicca.

**Yasodhara:** Siddhartha's wife and cousin.

**Yellow Ray:** The Third Ray, the Ray of Divine Wisdom, or "active intelligence."

**Ygraine:** Mother to King Arthur. First married to Gorlois, the Duke of Cornwall and later married to Uther Pendragon.

**Zarathustra:** Also known as Zoroaster. Founder of Zoroastrianism in Persia.

# About the Author

CHRISTOPHER PENCZAK is an award winning author, teacher and healing practitioner. As an advocate for the timeless perennial wisdom of the ages, he is rooted firmly in the traditions of modern Witchcraft and Earth based religions, but draws from a wide range of spiritual traditions including shamanism, alchemy, herbalism, Theosophy, and Hermetic Qabalah to forge his own magickal traditions. His many books include *Magick of Reiki, Spirit Allies, The Mystic Foundation,* and *The Inner Temple of Witchcraft.* He is the co-founder of the Temple of Witchcraft tradition, a nonprofit religious organization to advance the spiritual traditions of Witchcraft, as well as the co-founder of Copper Cauldron Publishing, a company dedicated to producing books, recordings, and tools for magickal inspiration and evolution. He has been a faculty member of the North Eastern Institute of Whole Health and a founding member of The Gifts of Grace, an interfaith foundation dedicated to acts of community service, both based in New Hampshire. He maintains a teaching and healing practice in New England, but travels extensively lecturing and teaching. More information can be found at *www.christopherpenczak.com*

CPSIA information can be obtained at www.ICGtesting.com
Printed in the USA
BVOW010203110712

294755BV00005B/5/P